Labor Force Characteristics by Race and Ethnicity, 2011

U.S. Department of Labor
Hilda L. Solis, Secretary

U.S. Bureau of Labor Statistics
John M. Galvin, Acting Commissioner

August 2012

Report 1036

Contents

Contents—continued

Labor Force Characteristics by Race and Ethnicity, 2011

Overview

In 2011, the unemployment rate for the United States averaged 8.9 percent, but varied across race and ethnicity groups. The rates were highest for Blacks (15.8 percent) and for American Indians and Alaska Natives (14.6 percent) and lowest for Whites (7.9 percent) and for Asians (7.0 percent). The jobless rate was 13.6 percent for persons of two or more races, 11.5 percent for Hispanics, and 10.4 percent for Native Hawaiians and Other Pacific Islanders.

Differences in labor force characteristics emerge when the race and ethnicity groups are compared. These differences reflect a variety of factors, not all of which are measurable. These factors include variations across the groups in educational attainment; the occupations and industries in which the groups work; the geographic areas of the country in which the groups are concentrated, including whether they tend to reside in urban or rural settings; and the degree of discrimination encountered in the workplace.

This report describes the labor force characteristics and earnings patterns among the major race and ethnicity groups—Whites, Blacks, Asians, and Hispanics—and provides more detailed data through a set of supporting tables. These data are obtained from the Current Population Survey (CPS), a monthly survey of 60,000 households that is a rich source of information on the labor force. For definitions of terms and concepts used in this report, see the Technical note. Additional information about the CPS can be found at **http://www.bls.gov/cps/documentation htm.**

For the first time, this report also includes a limited amount of data for American Indians, Alaska Natives, Native Hawaiians, Other Pacific Islanders, and for people who are of two or more races. Due to their relatively small sample size, estimates for these additional groups are not included in all tables. The following bullets highlight some of the major findings on the labor force characteristics of race and ethnicity groups in 2011.

Composition of the labor force

- By race, Whites made up the majority of the labor force in 2011 (81 percent). Blacks and Asians made up an additional 12 percent and 5 percent, respectively. American Indians and Alaska Natives composed about 1 percent of the labor force, as did persons of two or more races. Native Hawaiians and Other Pacific Islanders made up less than 1 percent. (See table 1.)

- By ethnicity, 15 percent of the labor force in 2011 were Hispanic or Latino. The majority of Hispanics in the labor force were Mexican (63 percent). The remainder consisted of Central and South Americans (25 percent), Puerto Ricans (8 percent), and Cubans (4 percent). (See table 2.)

- People of Hispanic ethnicity may be of any race. In 2011, the majority of Hispanics (93 percent) were White, 3 percent were Black, and 1 percent were Asian.

Labor force participation

- In 2011, American Indians and Alaska Natives (59.2 percent) and Blacks (61.4 percent) had the lowest labor force participation rates among the race and ethnicity groups, while Native Hawaiians and Other Pacific Islanders (69.4 percent) had the highest participation rates. The participation rates for Hispanics, Asians, and Whites, were 66.5 percent, 64.6 percent, and 64.5 percent, respectively. The participation rate for persons of two or more races was 64.0 percent in 2011. (See tables 1, 2, 3, and 4.)

- Among adult men (age 20 and over) in the major race and ethnicity groups, Blacks (68.4 percent) were less likely than other race and ethnicity groups to participate in the labor force. Hispanic men (81.7 percent) were more likely to participate in the labor force than other men. The labor force participation rate was 76.6 percent for Asian men and 73.9 percent for White men. (See table 3.)

- Among adult women, the proportions of White women (59.4 percent), Hispanic women (59.0 percent), and Asian women (58.7 percent) in the labor force were lower than that of Black women (62.2 percent).

Employment

- In 2011, the employment-population ratio (that is, the proportion of the population that is employed) ranged from 50.5 percent for American Indians and Alaska Natives to 62.2 percent for Native Hawaiians and Other Pacific Islanders. The employment-population ratio was 51.7 percent for Blacks, 55.3 percent for individuals of two or more races, 58.9 percent for Hispanics, 59.4 percent for Whites, and 60.0 percent for Asians. (See tables 1, 2, 3, and 5.)

- Among adult men (age 20 and older), Hispanics (73.3 percent) continued to have the highest employment-population ratio in 2011, followed by Asians (71.7 percent) and Whites (68.2 percent). The employment-population ratio for Black men, at 56.9 percent, was lower than the ratios for men in other groups in 2011, continuing a long-term pattern. Among adult women, Whites had the highest employment-population ratio, at 55.3 percent, followed by Asians (54.6 percent), and Blacks (54.0 percent). The ratio for Hispanic women (52.5 percent) continued to be lower than the ratio for other groups. (See table 3.)

- Among teenagers ages 16 to 19, the employment-population ratio was higher for Whites than for Hispanics, Asians, or Blacks. In 2011, the ratio for White teens (28.8 percent) was nearly twice that for Black teens (14.7 percent). The ratios for Hispanic and Asian teens were 19.5 percent and 16.2 percent, respectively.

Education

- Among people age 25 and older, the share of the labor force with at least a high school diploma was about 90 percent for Whites, Blacks, and Asians in 2011. By contrast, 69 percent of Hispanics in the labor force had completed high school. Asians were the most likely of the groups to have graduated from college; 57 percent of Asians in the labor force had a bachelor's degree or higher, compared with 36 percent of Whites, 25 percent of Blacks, and 16 percent of Hispanics. (See table 6.)

- For all major race and ethnicity groups, higher levels of education are generally associated with a greater likelihood of employment and a lower likelihood of unemployment. Individuals with higher levels of education generally have better access to higher paying jobs—such as those in management, professional, and related occupations—than do individuals with less education. However, at nearly every level of education, Blacks and Hispanics were more likely to be unemployed in 2011 than were Whites or Asians.

Occupation and industry

- The highest paying major occupational category is management, professional, and related occupations. In 2011, 47 percent of employed Asians worked in this occupational group, compared with 38 percent of employed Whites, 29 percent of employed Blacks, and 20 percent of employed Hispanics. (See table 7.)

- Among employed men, nearly half (49 percent) of Asians worked in management, professional, and related occupations in 2011, compared with 35 percent of Whites, 24 percent of Blacks, and 16 percent of Hispanics. About 2 in 10 employed Black and Hispanic men were employed in service occupations in 2011, whereas about 1 in 10 employed Asian and White men worked in these occupations. Employed Black and Hispanic men also were more likely than White or Asian men to work in production, transportation, and material moving occupations. About one-quarter of employed Hispanic men (26 percent) worked in natural resources, construction, and maintenance occupations, a higher share than for White men (18 percent), Black men (12 percent), or Asian men (7 percent).

- In 2011, employed Asian and White women were more likely than other women to work in management, professional, and related occupations—44 percent of Asian women and 42 percent of White women. By contrast, 34 percent of employed Black women and 25 percent of employed Hispanic women worked in this occupational group. Among employed women, 63 percent of Hispanics worked in either service occupations or sales and office occupations, compared with about 59 percent of Blacks, 52 percent of Whites, and 48 percent of Asians.

- In 2011, Hispanics accounted for 15 percent of total employment but were overrepresented by a substantial amount in several occupational categories, including miscellaneous agricultural workers (50 percent), roofers (47 percent), and packers and packagers (46 percent). Blacks made up 11 percent of all employed workers, but accounted for about one-quarter or more of those in several specific occupations, including nursing, psychiatric, and home health aides (33 percent); security guards (27 percent); and taxi drivers (27 percent). Asians accounted for 5 percent of all employed workers but made up a much larger share of workers in several occupational categories, including miscellaneous personal appearance workers (makeup artists, manicurists and pedicurists, shampooers, and skin care specialists; 55 percent), software developers (27 percent), and physicians and surgeons (16 percent). Whites made up 82 percent of all employed persons, but accounted for 96 percent of farmers, ranchers, and other agricultural managers; 95 percent of firefighters; and 94 percent of construction managers. (See table 8.)

- By industry, 18 percent of employed Hispanic men worked in construction in 2011, a larger share than White (12 percent), Black (7 percent), or Asian men (3 percent). Twelve percent of employed Black men worked in transportation and utilities, compared with 7 percent each of Hispanic and White men and

6 percent of Asian men. About 17 percent of employed Asian men worked in professional and business services, higher than the shares of their White (13 percent), Hispanic (12 percent), and Black (11 percent) counterparts. A large share of women in all race and ethnicity groups worked in education and health services in 2011—Blacks (42 percent), Whites (36 percent), Asians (31 percent), and Hispanics (30 percent). (See table 9.)

Families and mothers

- In 2011, 88 percent of Asian families had an employed family member, compared with 84 percent of Hispanic families and 80 percent of White families. Black families remained the least likely to have an employed family member (74 percent). (See table 10.)

- In 2011, nearly one-half (45 percent) of Black families and one-fourth (25 percent) of Hispanic families were maintained by women without a spouse present. About 16 percent of White families and 12 percent of Asian families were maintained by women. Among families maintained by women with no spouse present, Asian families were most likely to have an employed family member (81 percent), while Black families were the least likely to have an employed family member (67 percent). The proportion of White and Hispanic families that were maintained by women with an employed family member was 74 and 72 percent, respectively. In general, families maintained by women without a spouse present are less likely to have an employed member than other families.

- Among mothers with children under 18, Blacks were more likely to be in the labor force than Whites, Asians, or Hispanics. In 2011, 75.3 percent of Black mothers were labor force participants, compared with 70.2 percent of White mothers, 65.4 percent of Asian mothers, and 61.8 percent of Hispanic mothers. (See table 11.)

Unemployment and not in the labor force

- In 2011, unemployment rates among the race and ethnicity groups varied considerably by race and ethnicity. Blacks (15.8 percent) and American Indians and Alaska Natives (14.6 percent) had the highest unemployment rates, while Asians (7.0 percent) and Whites (7.9 percent) had the lowest. The unemployment rate was 11.5 percent for Hispanics, 10.4 percent for Native Hawaiians and Other Pacific Islanders, and 13.6 percent for individuals of two or more races. (See tables 1, 2, 3, and 12.)

- Among the major race and ethnicity groups, the jobless rates in 2011 for Black adult men and women (age 20 and older) were 16.7 and 13.2 percent, respectively. The unemployment rate for Hispanic adult men was 10.3 percent, and the rate for Hispanic adult women was 11.1 percent. In comparison, the unemployment rate for White adult men was 7.7 percent, and the rate for White adult women was 7.0 percent. The jobless rates for Asian adult men and women were 6.4 and 7.0 percent, respectively. (See table 3.)

- Black teenagers had the highest unemployment rate among the major race and ethnicity groups—41.3 percent in 2011. The unemployment rates for Hispanic, Asian, and White teenagers were 31.1 percent, 25.2 percent, and 21.7 percent, respectively.

- Unemployed Asians and Blacks experienced longer periods of unemployment than other workers. In 2011, the median duration of unemployment for Asians and Blacks was 27.7 weeks and 27.0 weeks, respectively, compared with 19.7 weeks for Whites and 18.5 weeks for Hispanics. (See table 13.)

- Of the 13.7 million unemployed persons in 2011, 59 percent (8.1 million) were job losers (that is, those workers who lost their jobs and those who completed temporary jobs). Reentrants to the labor force (25 percent), job leavers (7 percent), and new entrants (9 percent) constituted the balance of unemployed persons. Of the total unemployed for each major race and ethnicity group, about 60 percent of Whites and Hispanics were job losers in 2011, compared with 55 percent of Blacks and 53 percent of Asians. About 13 percent of Asians and 11 percent of Blacks and Hispanics were new entrants to the labor force in 2011, compared with nearly 9 percent of Whites. (See table 14.)

- In 2011, Blacks made up 12 percent of the civilian labor force, but 23 percent of persons marginally attached to the labor force. Persons marginally attached to the labor force are individuals who were not in the labor force, wanted and were available for work, and had looked for a job sometime in the previous 12 months—but not in the 4 weeks preceding the survey. Hispanics and Asians were represented among the marginally attached nearly proportionately to their shares of the labor force. Whites were underrepresented among the marginally attached relative to their share of the labor force. Blacks also composed a high proportion of discouraged workers (about 26 percent) in 2011. Discouraged workers, a subset of the marginally attached, are persons not currently looking for work because they believe no jobs are available for them. (See table 15.)

Earnings

- Among the major race and ethnicity groups, Hispanics and Blacks had considerably lower earnings than Asians and Whites. In 2011, the median usual weekly earnings of full-time wage and salary workers were $549 for Hispanics, $615 for Blacks, $775 for Whites, and $866 for Asians. Among men, the earnings of Whites ($856), Blacks ($653), and Hispanics ($571) were 88 percent, 67 percent, and 59 percent, respectively, of the earnings of Asians ($970). The median earnings of White women ($703), Black women ($595), and Hispanic women ($518) were 94, 79, and 69 percent, respectively, of the earnings of Asian women ($751). (See table 16.)

- For men, the earnings disparity across the major race and ethnicity groups holds for nearly all major occupational groups. For example, in 2011, median usual weekly earnings of Asian men ($1,414) and White men ($1,294) working full time in manage-

ment, professional, and related occupations (the highest paying major occupation group) were well above the earnings of Hispanic men ($1,019) and Black men ($965) in the same occupation group. Among those employed in management, professional, and related occupations, the earnings ratios of White, Hispanic, and Black men to Asian men were 92 percent, 72 percent, and 68 percent, respectively. In contrast, the earnings of White men employed full time in production, transportation, and material moving occupations were higher ($667) than the earnings of Black, Asian, and Hispanic men ($595, $584, and $525, respectively).

- Among the race and ethnicity groups, the earnings disparity was similar for women to that for men across the major occupational groups. For example, in production, transportation, and material moving occupations, the weekly earnings of White ($486) and Black ($490) women were about the same in 2011; the earnings of Asian and Hispanic women were $461 and $405 per week, respectively. In management, professional, and related occupations, the earnings of Asian women were higher than women of other race and ethnicity groups. In 2011, the earnings of White, Black, and Hispanic women were 84 percent, 74 percent, and 73 percent, respectively, of the earnings of Asian women.

Table 1. Employment status of the civilian noninstitutional population 16 years and older by sex and race, 2011 annual averages

(Numbers in thousands)

Sex and race	Civilian noninstitutional population	Civilian labor force							Not in labor force
		Total	Percent of population	Employed		Unemployed			
				Total	Percent of population	Total	Percent of labor force		
Total, both sexes	239,618	153,617	64.1	139,869	58.4	13,747	8.9		86,001
Men	116,317	81,975	70.5	74,290	63.9	7,684	9.4		34,343
Women	123,300	71,642	58.1	65,579	53.2	6,063	8.5		51,658
White, both sexes	193,077	124,579	64.5	114,690	59.4	9,889	7.9		68,498
Men	94,801	67,551	71.3	61,920	65.3	5,631	8.3		27,249
Women	98,276	57,028	58.0	52,770	53.7	4,257	7.5		41,248
Black or African American, both sexes	29,114	17,881	61.4	15,051	51.7	2,831	15.8		11,233
Men	13,164	8,454	64.2	6,953	52.8	1,502	17.8		4,710
Women	15,950	9,427	59.1	8,098	50.8	1,329	14.1		6,523
Asian, both sexes	11,439	7,386	64.6	6,867	60.0	518	7.0		4,054
Men	5,429	3,972	73.2	3,703	68.2	269	6.8		1,457
Women	6,011	3,414	56.8	3,165	52.6	250	7.3		2,596
American Indian and Alaska Native, both sexes	1,999	1,182	59.2	1,010	50.5	172	14.6		816
Men	989	645	65.2	546	55.2	99	15.4		344
Women	1,009	537	53.2	464	45.9	73	13.7		472
Native Hawaiian and Other Pacific Islander, both sexes	633	439	69.4	393	62.2	46	10.4		193
Men	308	232	75.6	206	67.0	26	11.4		75
Women	325	207	63.6	187	57.7	19	9.3		118
Two or more races, both sexes	3,356	2,149	64.0	1,857	55.3	292	13.6		1,207
Men	1,627	1,120	68.9	963	59.2	157	14.0		507
Women	1,730	1,029	59.5	895	51.7	135	13.1		701

Table 2. **Employment status of the civilian noninstitutional population by Hispanic or Latino ethnicity, sex, and race, 2011 annual averages**

(Numbers in thousands)

Hispanic or Latino ethnicity, sex, and race	Civilian noninstitutional population	Civilian labor force						Not in labor force
		Total	Percent of population	Employed		Unemployed		
				Total	Percent of population	Total	Percent of labor force	
Total, both sexes	239,618	153,617	64.1	139,869	58.4	13,747	8.9	86,001
Men	116,317	81,975	70.5	74,290	63.9	7,684	9.4	34,343
Women	123,300	71,642	58.1	65,579	53.2	6,063	8.5	51,658
Hispanic or Latino, both sexes	34,438	22,898	66.5	20,269	58.9	2,629	11.5	11,540
Men	17,753	13,576	76.5	12,049	67.9	1,527	11.2	4,177
Women	16,685	9,322	55.9	8,220	49.3	1,102	11.8	7,363
Mexican, both sexes	21,519	14,360	66.7	12,697	59.0	1,663	11.6	7,159
Men	11,321	8,841	78.1	7,850	69.3	991	11.2	2,480
Women	10,198	5,519	54.1	4,848	47.5	672	12.2	4,679
Puerto Rican, both sexes	3,201	1,893	59.2	1,627	50.8	266	14.1	1,307
Men	1,533	964	62.9	822	53.7	141	14.7	569
Women	1,668	930	55.7	805	48.2	125	13.5	738
Cuban, both sexes	1,533	976	63.6	867	56.5	109	11.2	558
Men	772	551	71.4	484	62.7	67	12.2	221
Women	761	424	55.8	383	50.3	42	9.8	337
Central and South American, both sexes	8,143	5,641	69.3	5,052	62.0	589	10.4	2,501
Men	4,111	3,205	78.0	2,879	70.0	326	10.2	906
Women	4,031	2,436	60.4	2,173	53.9	263	10.8	1,595
Other Hispanic or Latino, both sexes	42	27	63.6	25	59.7	2	–	15
Men	15	14	–	13	–	1	–	1
Women	27	12	–	12	–	1	–	14
Non-Hispanic or Latino, both sexes	205,180	130,719	63.7	119,600	58.3	11,119	8.5	74,461
Men	98,564	68,399	69.4	62,241	63.1	6,158	9.0	30,165
Women	106,616	62,320	58.5	57,359	53.8	4,961	8.0	44,295
White non-Hispanic or Latino, both sexes	161,158	103,334	64.1	95,846	59.5	7,488	7.2	57,824
Men	78,300	54,911	70.1	50,682	64.7	4,229	7.7	23,388
Women	82,858	48,423	58.4	45,164	54.5	3,259	6.7	34,435
Black non-Hispanic or Latino, both sexes	27,913	17,110	61.3	14,395	51.6	2,714	15.9	10,803
Men	12,606	8,051	63.9	6,609	52.4	1,442	17.9	4,555
Women	15,307	9,059	59.2	7,787	50.9	1,273	14.0	6,248
Asian non-Hispanic or Latino, both sexes	11,223	7,242	64.5	6,733	60.0	509	7.0	3,980
Men	5,320	3,892	73.2	3,629	68.2	264	6.8	1,427
Women	5,903	3,350	56.7	3,105	52.6	245	7.3	2,553

NOTE: Estimates for the above race groups (White non-Hispanic, Black non-Hispanic, and Asian non-Hispanic) do not sum to totals because data are not presented for all races. People whose ethnicity is identified as Hispanic or Latino may be of any race. Dash indicates no data or data that do not meet publication criteria (values not shown where base is less than 35,000).

Table 3. **Employment status of the civilian noninstitutional population by sex, age, race, and Hispanic or Latino ethnicity, 2011 annual averages**

(Numbers in thousands)

Age, sex, race, and Hispanic or Latino ethnicity	Civilian noninsti- tutional population	Civilian labor force						Not in labor force
		Total	Percent of population	Employed		Unemployed		
				Total	Percent of population	Total	Percent of labor force	
Total								
Total, 16 years and over	239,618	153,617	64.1	139,869	58.4	13,747	8.9	86,001
16 to 19 years	16,774	5,727	34.1	4,327	25.8	1,400	24.4	11,048
20 years and over	222,843	147,890	66.4	135,542	60.8	12,348	8.3	74,953
20 to 24 years	21,423	15,270	71.3	13,036	60.8	2,234	14.6	6,153
25 to 54 years	124,704	101,744	81.6	93,674	75.1	8,069	7.9	22,961
55 to 64 years	36,987	23,765	64.3	22,186	60.0	1,579	6.6	13,222
65 years and over	39,729	7,112	17.9	6,647	16.7	465	6.5	32,617
Men, 16 years and over	116,317	81,975	70.5	74,290	63.9	7,684	9.4	34,343
16 to 19 years	8,582	2,895	33.7	2,108	24.6	786	27.2	5,687
20 years and over	107,736	79,080	73.4	72,182	67.0	6,898	8.7	28,656
20 to 24 years	10,844	8,101	74.7	6,826	63.0	1,275	15.7	2,743
25 to 54 years	61,608	54,638	88.7	50,157	81.4	4,481	8.2	6,970
55 to 64 years	17,810	12,350	69.3	11,469	64.4	882	7.1	5,460
65 years and over	17,474	3,990	22.8	3,730	21.3	261	6.5	13,484
Women, 16 years and over	123,300	71,642	58.1	65,579	53.2	6,063	8.5	51,658
16 to 19 years	8,193	2,832	34.6	2,219	27.1	613	21.7	5,361
20 years and over	115,107	68,810	59.8	63,360	55.0	5,450	7.9	46,297
20 to 24 years	10,579	7,169	67.8	6,209	58.7	960	13.4	3,410
25 to 54 years	63,096	47,105	74.7	43,517	69.0	3,588	7.6	15,991
55 to 64 years	19,177	11,414	59.5	10,717	55.9	697	6.1	7,763
65 years and over	22,255	3,121	14.0	2,917	13.1	204	6.5	19,133
White								
Total, 16 years and over	193,077	124,579	64.5	114,690	59.4	9,889	7.9	68,498
16 to 19 years	12,818	4,714	36.8	3,691	28.8	1,024	21.7	8,103
20 years and over	180,259	119,865	66.5	111,000	61.6	8,865	7.4	60,394
20 to 24 years	16,562	12,120	73.2	10,574	63.8	1,546	12.8	4,442
25 to 54 years	98,692	81,381	82.5	75,708	76.7	5,673	7.0	17,311
55 to 64 years	30,799	20,188	65.5	18,937	61.5	1,251	6.2	10,610
65 years and over	34,206	6,175	18.1	5,780	16.9	395	6.4	28,031
Men, 16 years and over	94,801	67,551	71.3	61,920	65.3	5,631	8.3	27,249
16 to 19 years	6,610	2,386	36.1	1,802	27.3	585	24.5	4,223
20 years and over	88,191	65,165	73.9	60,118	68.2	5,046	7.7	23,026
20 to 24 years	8,485	6,539	77.1	5,630	66.4	909	13.9	1,946
25 to 54 years	49,474	44,502	90.0	41,285	83.4	3,217	7.2	4,972
55 to 64 years	15,018	10,629	70.8	9,932	66.1	697	6.6	4,389
65 years and over	15,213	3,494	23.0	3,271	21.5	223	6.4	11,719
Women, 16 years and over	98,276	57,028	58.0	52,770	53.7	4,257	7.5	41,248
16 to 19 years	6,208	2,328	37.5	1,889	30.4	439	18.9	3,880
20 years and over	92,068	54,700	59.4	50,881	55.3	3,818	7.0	37,368
20 to 24 years	8,077	5,581	69.1	4,943	61.2	637	11.4	2,496
25 to 54 years	49,218	36,879	74.9	34,423	69.9	2,456	6.7	12,339
55 to 64 years	15,781	9,559	60.6	9,005	57.1	554	5.8	6,221
65 years and over	18,992	2,681	14.1	2,509	13.2	171	6.4	16,312

See note at end of table.

7

Table 3. **Employment status of the civilian noninstitutional population by sex, age, race, and Hispanic or Latino ethnicity, 2011 annual averages—Continued**

(Levels in thousands)

Age, sex, race, and Hispanic or Latino ethnicity	Civilian noninsti-tutional population	Civilian labor force						Not in labor force
		Total	Percent of population	Employed		Unemployed		
				Total	Percent of population	Total	Percent of labor force	
Black or African American								
Total, 16 years and over	29,114	17,881	61.4	15,051	51.7	2,831	15.8	11,233
16 to 19 years	2,594	647	24.9	380	14.7	267	41.3	1,947
20 years and over	26,520	17,234	65.0	14,671	55.3	2,564	14.9	9,286
20 to 24 years	3,168	2,105	66.5	1,574	49.7	531	25.2	1,063
25 to 54 years	15,958	12,420	77.8	10,645	66.7	1,775	14.3	3,539
55 to 64 years	3,955	2,155	54.5	1,943	49.1	212	9.8	1,800
65 years and over	3,440	555	16.1	508	14.8	47	8.4	2,885
Men, 16 years and over	13,164	8,454	64.2	6,953	52.8	1,502	17.8	4,710
16 to 19 years	1,282	329	25.7	187	14.6	142	43.1	953
20 years and over	11,882	8,125	68.4	6,765	56.9	1,360	16.7	3,757
20 to 24 years	1,510	1,012	67.0	734	48.6	278	27.4	498
25 to 54 years	7,269	5,872	80.8	4,937	67.9	935	15.9	1,397
55 to 64 years	1,759	983	55.9	858	48.8	125	12.7	775
65 years and over	1,344	257	19.1	236	17.5	21	8.2	1,087
Women, 16 years and over	15,950	9,427	59.1	8,098	50.8	1,329	14.1	6,523
16 to 19 years	1,312	318	24.2	193	14.7	125	39.4	994
20 years and over	14,638	9,110	62.2	7,906	54.0	1,204	13.2	5,529
20 to 24 years	1,657	1,093	65.9	840	50.7	253	23.1	565
25 to 54 years	8,689	6,547	75.4	5,708	65.7	839	12.8	2,142
55 to 64 years	2,196	1,172	53.4	1,086	49.4	86	7.4	1,024
65 years and over	2,096	298	14.2	272	13.0	25	8.5	1,798
Asian								
Total, 16 years and over	11,439	7,386	64.6	6,867	60.0	518	7.0	4,054
16 to 19 years	652	141	21.7	106	16.2	36	25.2	510
20 years and over	10,788	7,244	67.2	6,762	62.7	483	6.7	3,543
20 to 24 years	940	518	55.1	461	49.1	57	11.0	421
25 to 54 years	6,789	5,428	80.0	5,097	75.1	332	6.1	1,360
55 to 64 years	1,555	1,032	66.3	953	61.3	78	7.6	524
65 years and over	1,504	266	17.7	250	16.6	16	6.0	1,238
Men, 16 years and over	5,429	3,972	73.2	3,703	68.2	269	6.8	1,457
16 to 19 years	331	66	20.1	46	13.9	20	30.5	265
20 years and over	5,098	3,905	76.6	3,657	71.7	249	6.4	1,193
20 to 24 years	472	269	57.1	238	50.4	32	11.7	203
25 to 54 years	3,255	2,936	90.2	2,768	85.1	168	5.7	319
55 to 64 years	707	531	75.0	492	69.6	39	7.3	177
65 years and over	663	169	25.5	158	23.9	11	6.4	494
Women, 16 years and over	6,011	3,414	56.8	3,165	52.6	250	7.3	2,596
16 to 19 years	321	75	23.4	60	18.6	15	20.5	246
20 years and over	5,690	3,339	58.7	3,105	54.6	234	7.0	2,351
20 to 24 years	467	249	53.2	223	47.8	25	10.1	219
25 to 54 years	3,534	2,493	70.5	2,329	65.9	164	6.6	1,041
55 to 64 years	848	501	59.1	461	54.4	40	7.9	347
65 years and over	841	97	11.6	92	10.9	5	5.3	744

See note at end of table.

Table 3. **Employment status of the civilian noninstitutional population by sex, age, race, and Hispanic or Latino ethnicity, 2011 annual averages—Continued**

(Levels in thousands)

Age, sex, race, and Hispanic or Latino ethnicity	Civilian noninsti- tutional population	Civilian labor force						Not in labor force
		Total	Percent of population	Employed		Unemployed		
				Total	Percent of population	Total	Percent of labor force	
Hispanic or Latino ethnicity								
Total, 16 years and over	34,438	22,898	66.5	20,269	58.9	2,629	11.5	11,540
16 to 19 years	3,407	965	28.3	665	19.5	300	31.1	2,442
20 years and over	31,031	21,933	70.7	19,604	63.2	2,329	10.6	9,098
20 to 24 years	4,193	3,017	72.0	2,544	60.7	473	15.7	1,175
25 to 54 years	20,624	16,390	79.5	14,774	71.6	1,616	9.9	4,234
55 to 64 years	3,311	2,015	60.8	1,820	55.0	195	9.7	1,296
65 years and over	2,903	511	17.6	465	16.0	45	8.8	2,393
Men, 16 years and over	17,753	13,576	76.5	12,049	67.9	1,527	11.2	4,177
16 to 19 years	1,812	545	30.1	364	20.1	182	33.3	1,266
20 years and over	15,941	13,030	81.7	11,685	73.3	1,345	10.3	2,911
20 to 24 years	2,278	1,811	79.5	1,535	67.4	277	15.3	467
25 to 54 years	10,799	9,803	90.8	8,880	82.2	924	9.4	996
55 to 64 years	1,604	1,122	69.9	1,006	62.7	116	10.4	482
65 years and over	1,260	293	23.3	266	21.1	28	9.5	966
Women, 16 years and over	16,685	9,322	55.9	8,220	49.3	1,102	11.8	7,363
16 to 19 years	1,595	419	26.3	301	18.9	118	28.1	1,176
20 years and over	15,090	8,902	59.0	7,918	52.5	984	11.1	6,187
20 to 24 years	1,915	1,206	63.0	1,010	52.7	196	16.3	709
25 to 54 years	9,825	6,587	67.0	5,894	60.0	692	10.5	3,238
55 to 64 years	1,707	893	52.3	814	47.7	78	8.8	814
65 years and over	1,643	217	13.2	200	12.1	17	8.0	1,426

NOTE: Estimates for the above race groups (White, Black or African American, and Asian) do not sum to totals because data are not presented for all races. People whose ethnicity is identified as Hispanic or Latino may be of any race.

Table 4. **Labor force participation rates by sex, race, and Hispanic or Latino ethnicity, 1972–2011 annual averages**

(Percent)

Year	Total			White			Black or African American			Asian			Hispanic or Latino ethnicity		
	Total	Men	Women	Total	Men	Women	Total	Men	Women	Total	Men	Women	Total	Men	Women
1972	60.4	78.9	43.9	60.4	79.6	43.2	59.9	73.6	48.7	—	—	—	—	—	—
1973	60.8	78.8	44.7	60.8	79.4	44.1	60.2	73.4	49.3	—	—	—	60.2	81.5	41.0
1974	61.3	78.7	45.7	61.4	79.4	45.2	59.8	72.9	49.0	—	—	—	61.1	81.7	42.4
1975	61.2	77.9	46.3	61.5	78.7	45.9	58.8	70.9	48.8	—	—	—	60.8	80.7	43.2
1976	61.6	77.5	47.3	61.8	78.4	46.9	59.0	70.0	49.8	—	—	—	60.8	79.6	44.3
1977	62.3	77.7	48.4	62.5	78.5	48.0	59.8	70.6	50.8	—	—	—	61.6	80.9	44.3
1978	63.2	77.9	50.0	63.3	78.6	49.4	61.5	71.5	53.1	—	—	—	62.9	81.1	46.6
1979	63.7	77.8	50.9	63.9	78.6	50.5	61.4	71.3	53.1	—	—	—	63.6	81.3	47.4
1980	63.8	77.4	51.5	64.1	78.2	51.2	61.0	70.3	53.1	—	—	—	64.0	81.4	47.4
1981	63.9	77.0	52.1	64.3	77.9	51.9	60.8	70.0	53.5	—	—	—	64.1	80.6	48.3
1982	64.0	76.6	52.6	64.3	77.4	52.4	61.0	70.1	53.7	—	—	—	63.6	79.7	48.1
1983	64.0	76.4	52.9	64.3	77.1	52.7	61.5	70.6	54.2	—	—	—	63.8	80.3	47.7
1984	64.4	76.4	53.6	64.6	77.1	53.3	62.2	70.8	55.2	—	—	—	64.9	80.6	49.7
1985	64.8	76.3	54.5	65.0	77.0	54.1	62.9	70.8	56.5	—	—	—	64.6	80.4	49.3
1986	65.3	76.3	55.3	65.5	76.9	55.0	63.3	71.2	56.9	—	—	—	65.4	81.0	50.1
1987	65.6	76.2	56.0	65.8	76.8	55.7	63.8	71.1	58.0	—	—	—	66.4	81.0	52.0
1988	65.9	76.2	56.6	66.2	76.9	56.4	63.8	71.0	58.0	—	—	—	67.4	81.9	53.2
1989	66.5	76.4	57.4	66.7	77.1	57.2	64.2	71.0	58.7	—	—	—	67.6	82.0	53.5
1990	66.5	76.4	57.5	66.9	77.1	57.4	64.0	71.0	58.3	—	—	—	67.4	81.4	53.1
1991	66.2	75.8	57.4	66.6	76.5	57.4	63.3	70.4	57.5	—	—	—	66.5	80.3	52.4
1992	66.4	75.8	57.8	66.8	76.5	57.7	63.9	70.7	58.5	—	—	—	66.8	80.7	52.8
1993	66.3	75.4	57.9	66.8	76.2	58.0	63.2	69.6	57.9	—	—	—	66.2	80.2	52.1
1994	66.6	75.1	58.8	67.1	75.9	58.9	63.4	69.1	58.7	—	—	—	66.1	79.2	52.9
1995	66.6	75.0	58.9	67.1	75.7	59.0	63.7	69.0	59.5	—	—	—	65.8	79.1	52.6
1996	66.8	74.9	59.3	67.2	75.8	59.1	64.1	68.7	60.4	—	—	—	66.5	79.6	53.4
1997	67.1	75.0	59.8	67.5	75.9	59.5	64.7	68.3	61.7	—	—	—	67.9	80.1	55.1
1998	67.1	74.9	59.8	67.3	75.6	59.4	65.6	69.0	62.8	—	—	—	67.9	79.8	55.6
1999	67.1	74.7	60.0	67.3	75.6	59.6	65.8	68.7	63.5	—	—	—	67.7	79.8	55.9
2000	67.1	74.8	59.9	67.3	75.5	59.5	65.8	69.2	63.1	67.2	76.1	59.2	69.7	81.5	57.5
2001	66.8	74.4	59.8	67.0	75.1	59.4	65.3	68.4	62.8	67.2	76.2	59.0	69.5	81.0	57.6
2002	66.6	74.1	59.6	66.8	74.8	59.3	64.8	68.4	61.8	67.2	75.9	59.1	69.1	80.2	57.6
2003	66.2	73.5	59.5	66.5	74.2	59.2	64.3	67.3	61.9	66.4	75.6	58.3	68.3	80.1	55.9
2004	66.0	73.3	59.2	66.3	74.1	58.9	63.8	66.7	61.5	65.9	75.0	57.6	68.6	80.4	56.1
2005	66.0	73.3	59.3	66.3	74.1	58.9	64.2	67.3	61.6	66.1	74.8	58.2	68.0	80.1	55.3
2006	66.2	73.5	59.4	66.5	74.3	59.0	64.1	67.0	61.7	66.2	75.0	58.3	68.7	80.7	56.1
2007	66.0	73.2	59.3	66.4	74.0	59.0	63.7	66.8	61.1	66.5	75.1	58.6	68.8	80.5	56.5
2008	66.0	73.0	59.5	66.3	73.7	59.2	63.7	66.7	61.3	67.0	75.3	59.4	68.5	80.2	56.2
2009	65.4	72.0	59.2	65.8	72.8	59.1	62.4	65.0	60.3	66.0	74.6	58.2	68.0	78.8	56.5
2010	64.7	71.2	58.6	65.1	72.0	58.5	62.2	65.0	59.9	64.7	73.2	57.0	67.5	77.8	56.5
2011	64.1	70.5	58.1	64.5	71.3	58.0	61.4	64.2	59.1	64.6	73.2	56.8	66.5	76.5	55.9

See note at end of table.

Table 4. **Labor force participation rates by sex, race, and Hispanic or Latino ethnicity, 1972–2011 annual averages—Continued**

(Percent)

Year	American Indian and Alaska Native			Native Hawaiian and Other Pacific Islander			Two or more races		
	Total	Men	Women	Total	Men	Women	Total	Men	Women
2003	64.4	71.0	58.0	68.9	75.0	63.9	67.6	73.2	62.4
2004	63.8	70.9	57.1	71.8	76.6	67.7	67.0	74.0	60.3
2005	63.5	70.0	57.2	73.4	77.1	69.8	67.0	72.0	62.3
2006	63.1	68.6	57.9	74.5	80.8	68.6	65.9	72.3	59.7
2007	63.3	69.9	57.0	73.0	78.4	68.2	66.3	71.9	60.8
2008	63.7	70.2	57.6	72.5	78.9	66.6	65.5	70.7	60.4
2009	59.0	64.1	54.2	69.4	77.3	62.3	65.6	70.4	61.0
2010	57.7	64.0	51.8	68.4	71.3	65.5	65.4	70.9	60.3
2011	59.2	65.2	53.2	69.4	75.6	63.6	64.0	68.9	59.5

NOTE: Beginning in 2003, estimates for White, Black or African American, Asian, American Indian and Alaska Native, and Native Hawaiian and Other Pacific Islander race groups include people who selected that race group only; people who selected more than one race group are included in the two or more races category. Prior to 2003, people who reported more than one race were included in the group they identified as their main race. Asian estimates for 2000–2002 include Asians and Pacific Islanders; beginning in 2003, Asian is a separate category, as is Native Hawaiian and Other Pacific Islander. People whose ethnicity is identified as Hispanic or Latino may be of any race. Dash indicates data not available.

Table 5. **Employment-population ratios by sex, race, and Hispanic or Latino ethnicity, 1972–2011 annual averages**

(Percent)

Year	Total			White			Black or African American			Asian			Hispanic or Latino ethnicity		
	Total	Men	Women	Total	Men	Women	Total	Men	Women	Total	Men	Women	Total	Men	Women
1972	57.0	75.0	41.0	57.4	76.0	40.7	53.7	66.8	43.0	—	—	—	—	—	—
1973	57.8	75.5	42.0	58.2	76.5	41.8	54.5	67.5	43.8	—	—	—	55.6	76.0	37.3
1974	57.8	74.9	42.6	58.3	75.9	42.4	53.5	65.8	43.5	—	—	—	56.2	75.7	38.4
1975	56.1	71.7	42.0	56.7	73.0	42.0	50.1	60.6	41.6	—	—	—	53.4	71.5	37.4
1976	56.8	72.0	43.2	57.5	73.4	43.2	50.8	60.6	42.8	—	—	—	53.8	71.1	38.6
1977	57.9	72.8	44.5	58.6	74.1	44.5	51.4	61.4	43.3	—	—	—	55.4	73.6	39.1
1978	59.3	73.8	46.4	60.0	75.0	46.3	53.6	63.3	45.8	—	—	—	57.2	74.9	41.3
1979	59.9	73.8	47.5	60.6	75.1	47.5	53.8	63.4	46.0	—	—	—	58.3	75.6	42.5
1980	59.2	72.0	47.7	60.0	73.4	47.8	52.3	60.4	45.7	—	—	—	57.6	73.5	42.4
1981	59.0	71.3	48.0	60.0	72.8	48.3	51.3	59.1	45.1	—	—	—	57.4	72.4	43.0
1982	57.8	69.0	47.7	58.8	70.6	48.1	49.4	56.0	44.2	—	—	—	54.9	68.9	41.3
1983	57.9	68.8	48.0	58.9	70.4	48.5	49.5	56.3	44.1	—	—	—	55.1	69.4	41.1
1984	59.5	70.7	49.5	60.5	72.1	49.8	52.3	59.2	46.7	—	—	—	57.9	72.1	44.2
1985	60.1	70.9	50.4	61.0	72.3	50.7	53.4	60.0	48.1	—	—	—	57.8	72.1	43.8
1986	60.7	71.0	51.4	61.5	72.3	51.7	54.1	60.6	48.8	—	—	—	58.5	72.5	44.7
1987	61.5	71.5	52.5	62.3	72.7	52.8	55.6	62.0	50.3	—	—	—	60.5	74.0	47.4
1988	62.3	72.0	53.4	63.1	73.2	53.8	56.3	62.7	51.2	—	—	—	61.9	75.3	48.8
1989	63.0	72.5	54.3	63.8	73.7	54.6	56.9	62.8	52.0	—	—	—	62.2	75.8	48.8
1990	62.8	72.0	54.3	63.7	73.3	54.7	56.7	62.6	51.9	—	—	—	61.9	74.9	48.6
1991	61.7	70.4	53.7	62.6	71.6	54.2	55.4	61.3	50.6	—	—	—	59.8	72.1	47.3
1992	61.5	69.8	53.8	62.4	71.1	54.2	54.9	59.9	50.8	—	—	—	59.1	71.2	46.8
1993	61.7	70.0	54.1	62.7	71.4	54.6	55.0	60.0	50.9	—	—	—	59.1	71.7	46.3
1994	62.5	70.4	55.3	63.5	71.8	55.8	56.1	60.8	52.3	—	—	—	59.5	71.7	47.2
1995	62.9	70.8	55.6	63.8	72.0	56.1	57.1	61.7	53.4	—	—	—	59.7	72.1	47.3
1996	63.2	70.9	56.0	64.1	72.3	56.3	57.4	61.1	54.4	—	—	—	60.6	73.3	47.9
1997	63.8	71.3	56.8	64.6	72.7	57.0	58.2	61.4	55.6	—	—	—	62.6	74.5	50.2
1998	64.1	71.6	57.1	64.7	72.7	57.1	59.7	62.9	57.2	—	—	—	63.1	74.7	51.0
1999	64.3	71.6	57.4	64.8	72.8	57.3	60.6	63.1	58.6	—	—	—	63.4	75.3	51.7
2000	64.4	71.9	57.5	64.9	73.0	57.4	60.9	63.6	58.6	64.8	73.3	57.1	65.7	77.4	53.6
2001	63.7	70.9	57.0	64.2	72.0	57.0	59.7	62.1	57.8	64.2	72.7	56.4	64.9	76.2	53.3
2002	62.7	69.7	56.3	63.4	70.8	56.4	58.1	61.1	55.8	63.2	71.3	55.8	63.9	74.5	52.9
2003	62.3	68.9	56.1	63.0	70.1	56.3	57.4	59.5	55.6	62.4	70.9	54.9	63.1	74.3	51.2
2004	62.3	69.2	56.0	63.1	70.4	56.1	57.2	59.3	55.5	63.0	71.6	55.1	63.8	75.1	51.8
2005	62.7	69.6	56.2	63.4	70.8	56.3	57.7	60.2	55.7	63.4	71.8	55.9	64.0	75.8	51.5
2006	63.1	70.1	56.6	63.8	71.3	56.6	58.4	60.6	56.5	64.2	72.7	56.5	65.2	76.8	52.8
2007	63.0	69.8	56.6	63.6	70.9	56.7	58.4	60.7	56.5	64.3	72.8	56.6	64.9	76.2	53.0
2008	62.2	68.5	56.2	62.8	69.7	56.3	57.3	59.1	55.8	64.3	72.2	57.2	63.3	74.1	51.9
2009	59.3	64.5	54.4	60.2	66.0	54.8	53.2	53.7	52.8	61.2	68.7	54.4	59.7	68.9	50.1
2010	58.5	63.7	53.6	59.4	65.1	54.0	52.3	53.1	51.7	59.9	67.5	53.0	59.0	68.0	49.6
2011	58.4	63.9	53.2	59.4	65.3	53.7	51.7	52.8	50.8	60.0	68.2	52.6	58.9	67.9	49.3

See note at end of table.

Table 5. **Employment-population ratios by sex, race, and Hispanic or Latino ethnicity, 1972–2011 annual averages—Continued**

(Percent)

Year	American Indian and Alaska Native			Native Hawaiian and Other Pacific Islander			Two or more races		
	Total	Men	Women	Total	Men	Women	Total	Men	Women
2003	57.7	63.1	52.4	63.6	69.8	58.4	61.4	66.4	56.8
2004	57.7	64.0	51.8	67.4	71.4	64.1	61.2	67.6	55.0
2005	57.6	63.9	51.5	70.2	73.4	67.1	61.6	66.3	57.2
2006	58.1	63.2	53.3	70.6	75.7	65.7	61.5	67.0	56.2
2007	58.1	64.3	52.3	69.4	74.2	65.3	61.5	66.5	56.6
2008	57.4	62.6	52.5	67.8	72.8	63.3	59.3	63.6	55.2
2009	51.2	54.2	48.3	61.8	68.3	56.0	56.7	60.4	53.2
2010	49.0	53.0	45.2	60.1	61.6	58.7	56.5	60.8	52.5
2011	50.5	55.2	45.9	62.2	67.0	57.7	55.3	59.2	51.7

NOTE: Beginning in 2003, estimates for White, Black or African American, Asian, American Indian and Alaska Native, and Native Hawaiian and Other Pacific Islander race groups include people who selected that race group only; people who selected more than one race group are included in the two or more races category. Prior to 2003, people who reported more than one race were included in the group they identified as their main race. Asian estimates for 2000–2002 include Asians and Pacific Islanders; beginning in 2003, Asian is a separate category, as is Native Hawaiian and Other Pacific Islander. People whose ethnicity is identified as Hispanic or Latino may be of any race. Dash indicates data not available.

Table 6. **Employment status of people 25 years and older by educational attainment, sex, race, and Hispanic or Latino ethnicity, 2011 annual averages**

(Numbers in thousands)

Employment status, sex, race, and Hispanic or Latino ethnicity	Total, 25 years and older	Less than a high school diploma	High school graduates, no college[1]	Some college, no degree	Associate degree	Bachelor's degree and higher[2]
TOTAL						
Civilian noninstitutional population	201,420	25,122	61,932	33,898	19,191	61,277
Civilian labor force	132,620	11,599	37,344	22,686	14,145	46,846
Percent of population	65.8	46.2	60.3	66.9	73.7	76.4
Employed	122,507	9,967	33,823	20,712	13,182	44,822
Employment-population ratio	60.8	39.7	54.6	61.1	68.7	73.1
Unemployed	10,113	1,632	3,521	1,974	963	2,024
Unemployment rate	7.6	14.1	9.4	8.7	6.8	4.3
Men						
Civilian noninstitutional population	96,892	12,563	30,264	16,078	8,229	29,758
Civilian labor force	70,979	7,398	21,169	11,760	6,469	24,183
Percent of population	73.3	58.9	69.9	73.1	78.6	81.3
Employed	65,356	6,388	19,059	10,741	6,029	23,138
Employment-population ratio	67.5	50.9	63.0	66.8	73.3	77.8
Unemployed	5,623	1,009	2,110	1,018	440	1,045
Unemployment rate	7.9	13.6	10.0	8.7	6.8	4.3
Women						
Civilian noninstitutional population	104,528	12,559	31,668	17,820	10,962	31,519
Civilian labor force	61,641	4,201	16,175	10,926	7,676	22,663
Percent of population	59.0	33.5	51.1	61.3	70.0	71.9
Employed	57,151	3,579	14,764	9,971	7,153	21,684
Employment-population ratio	54.7	28.5	46.6	56.0	65.3	68.8
Unemployed	4,490	623	1,411	955	523	978
Unemployment rate	7.3	14.8	8.7	8.7	6.8	4.3
WHITE						
Civilian noninstitutional population	163,696	19,765	50,280	27,370	15,765	50,516
Civilian labor force	107,745	9,443	30,093	18,109	11,609	38,492
Percent of population	65.8	47.8	59.8	66.2	73.6	76.2
Employed	100,426	8,248	27,568	16,713	10,922	36,975
Employment-population ratio	61.3	41.7	54.8	61.1	69.3	73.2
Unemployed	7,318	1,195	2,524	1,396	687	1,516
Unemployment rate	6.8	12.7	8.4	7.7	5.9	3.9
Men						
Civilian noninstitutional population	79,706	10,110	24,704	13,141	6,865	24,885
Civilian labor force	58,625	6,211	17,317	9,590	5,399	20,108
Percent of population	73.6	61.4	70.1	73.0	78.7	80.8
Employed	54,488	5,450	15,776	8,878	5,082	19,303
Employment-population ratio	68.4	53.9	63.9	67.6	74.0	77.6
Unemployed	4,137	762	1,541	712	318	805
Unemployment rate	7.1	12.3	8.9	7.4	5.9	4.0
Women						
Civilian noninstitutional population	83,991	9,655	25,576	14,229	8,900	25,630
Civilian labor force	49,119	3,232	12,776	8,518	6,210	18,384
Percent of population	58.5	33.5	50.0	59.9	69.8	71.7
Employed	45,938	2,798	11,792	7,835	5,840	17,672
Employment-population ratio	54.7	29.0	46.1	55.1	65.6	69.0
Unemployed	3,181	433	984	683	369	711
Unemployment rate	6.5	13.4	7.7	8.0	5.9	3.9

See footnotes at end of table.

Table 6. **Employment status of people 25 years and older by educational attainment, sex, race, and Hispanic or Latino ethnicity, 2011 annual averages—Continued**

(Levels in thousands)

Employment status, sex, race, and Hispanic or Latino ethnicity	Total, 25 years and older	Less than a high school diploma	High school graduates, no college[1]	Some college, no degree	Associate degree	Bachelor's degree and higher[2]
BLACK OR AFRICAN AMERICAN						
Civilian noninstitutional population	23,353	3,545	8,176	4,563	2,314	4,755
Civilian labor force	15,129	1,343	5,088	3,233	1,727	3,738
Percent of population	64.8	37.9	62.2	70.8	74.6	78.6
Employed	13,097	1,013	4,298	2,792	1,519	3,474
Employment-population ratio	56.1	28.6	52.6	61.2	65.6	73.1
Unemployed	2,033	330	790	440	208	264
Unemployment rate	13.4	24.6	15.5	13.6	12.1	7.1
Men						
Civilian noninstitutional population	10,372	1,638	3,953	1,973	880	1,929
Civilian labor force	7,112	717	2,676	1,462	684	1,573
Percent of population	68.6	43.8	67.7	74.1	77.8	81.6
Employed	6,031	532	2,225	1,235	591	1,449
Employment-population ratio	58.1	32.5	56.3	62.6	67.2	75.1
Unemployed	1,082	185	451	228	93	124
Unemployment rate	15.2	25.9	16.9	15.6	13.6	7.9
Women						
Civilian noninstitutional population	12,981	1,907	4,223	2,590	1,435	2,826
Civilian labor force	8,017	626	2,412	1,770	1,043	2,165
Percent of population	61.8	32.8	57.1	68.3	72.7	76.6
Employed	7,066	481	2,073	1,558	928	2,026
Employment-population ratio	54.4	25.2	49.1	60.1	64.7	71.7
Unemployed	951	145	339	212	115	140
Unemployment rate	11.9	23.1	14.0	12.0	11.1	6.4
ASIAN						
Civilian noninstitutional population	9,848	1,097	2,072	1,015	637	5,027
Civilian labor force	6,726	463	1,265	707	460	3,831
Percent of population	68.3	42.2	61.1	69.6	72.2	76.2
Employed	6,300	419	1,169	650	430	3,632
Employment-population ratio	64.0	38.2	56.4	64.0	67.6	72.2
Unemployed	426	44	96	57	30	199
Unemployment rate	6.3	9.5	7.6	8.0	6.5	5.2
Men						
Civilian noninstitutional population	4,626	441	880	517	281	2,506
Civilian labor force	3,636	249	647	382	228	2,129
Percent of population	78.6	56.6	73.5	73.9	81.0	85.0
Employed	3,419	226	596	346	215	2,035
Employment-population ratio	73.9	51.2	67.8	67.0	76.6	81.2
Unemployed	217	24	51	36	12	94
Unemployment rate	6.0	9.5	7.8	9.3	5.4	4.4
Women						
Civilian noninstitutional population	5,223	656	1,192	498	355	2,521
Civilian labor force	3,091	214	618	325	232	1,702
Percent of population	59.2	32.6	51.9	65.2	65.3	67.5
Employed	2,882	193	573	304	215	1,597
Employment-population ratio	55.2	29.5	48.0	60.9	60.4	63.4
Unemployed	209	20	45	21	17	105
Unemployment rate	6.8	9.6	7.3	6.5	7.5	6.2

See footnotes at end of table.

Table 6. **Employment status of people 25 years and older by educational attainment, sex, race, and Hispanic or Latino ethnicity, 2011 annual averages—Continued**

(Levels in thousands)

Employment status, sex, race, and Hispanic or Latino ethnicity	Total, 25 years and older	Less than a high school diploma	High school graduates, no college[1]	Some college, no degree	Associate degree	Bachelor's degree and higher[2]
HISPANIC OR LATINO ETHNICITY						
Civilian noninstitutional population	26,838	9,612	8,000	3,622	1,844	3,761
Civilian labor force	18,915	5,859	5,813	2,770	1,444	3,030
Percent of population	70.5	61.0	72.7	76.5	78.3	80.6
Employed	17,059	5,156	5,216	2,513	1,317	2,857
Employment-population ratio	63.6	53.6	65.2	69.4	71.4	76.0
Unemployed	1,856	703	597	257	127	173
Unemployment rate	9.8	12.0	10.3	9.3	8.8	5.7
Men						
Civilian noninstitutional population	13,663	5,021	4,213	1,798	810	1,821
Civilian labor force	11,219	3,919	3,519	1,512	689	1,580
Percent of population	82.1	78.1	83.5	84.1	85.1	86.8
Employed	10,151	3,487	3,158	1,377	636	1,492
Employment-population ratio	74.3	69.5	74.9	76.6	78.6	81.9
Unemployed	1,068	432	361	134	53	88
Unemployment rate	9.5	11.0	10.3	8.9	7.7	5.6
Women						
Civilian noninstitutional population	13,175	4,591	3,787	1,824	1,034	1,939
Civilian labor force	7,696	1,939	2,294	1,258	754	1,450
Percent of population	58.4	42.2	60.6	69.0	73.0	74.8
Employed	6,908	1,669	2,058	1,136	681	1,365
Employment-population ratio	52.4	36.3	54.4	62.3	65.8	70.4
Unemployed	788	271	235	123	74	86
Unemployment rate	10.2	14.0	10.3	9.7	9.8	5.9

[1] Includes people with a high school diploma or equivalent.

[2] Includes people with bachelor's, master's, professional, and doctoral degrees.

NOTE: Estimates for the above race groups (White, Black or African American, and Asian) do not sum to totals because data are not presented for all races. People whose ethnicity is identified as Hispanic or Latino may be of any race.

Table 7. **Employed people by occupation, sex, race, and Hispanic or Latino ethnicity, 2011 annual averages**

Occupation and sex	Total	White	Black or African American	Asian	Hispanic or Latino ethnicity
Total, 16 years and older (thousands)	139,869	114,690	15,051	6,867	20,269
Percent	100.0	100.0	100.0	100.0	100.0
Management, professional, and related occupations	37.6	38.3	29.2	46.9	19.5
Management, business, and financial operations occupations	15.4	16.1	10.5	16.2	8.2
Management occupations	10.9	11.6	6.4	10.1	5.8
Business and financial operations occupations	4.5	4.5	4.1	6.1	2.4
Professional and related occupations	22.1	22.2	18.7	30.8	11.3
Computer and mathematical occupations	2.6	2.3	1.7	8.7	1.0
Architecture and engineering occupations	2.0	2.1	1.0	3.6	0.9
Life, physical, and social science occupations	0.9	0.9	0.6	1.9	0.4
Community and social service occupations	1.7	1.6	2.8	1.0	1.2
Legal occupations	1.3	1.3	0.9	1.0	0.5
Education, training, and library occupations	6.2	6.4	5.5	4.4	3.5
Arts, design, entertainment, sports, and media occupations	2.0	2.1	1.1	1.5	1.2
Healthcare practitioner and technical occupations	5.5	5.4	5.1	8.7	2.6
Service occupations	17.7	16.6	25.4	17.7	25.7
Healthcare support occupations	2.4	2.0	5.5	2.1	2.3
Protective service occupations	2.3	2.2	3.7	1.0	2.0
Food preparation and serving related occupations	5.5	5.3	6.5	6.6	8.3
Building and grounds cleaning and maintenance occupations	3.9	3.9	5.0	2.4	9.4
Personal care and service occupations	3.6	3.3	4.7	5.5	3.6
Sales and office occupations	23.6	23.6	24.9	21.3	21.6
Sales and related occupations	11.0	11.1	10.0	10.8	9.5
Office and administrative support occupations	12.7	12.5	14.9	10.5	12.0
Natural resources, construction, and maintenance occupations	9.3	10.1	5.6	3.8	16.3
Farming, fishing, and forestry occupations	0.7	0.8	0.3	0.2	2.1
Construction and extraction occupations	5.1	5.6	2.8	1.5	10.3
Installation, maintenance, and repair occupations	3.5	3.7	2.6	2.0	3.8
Production, transportation, and material moving occupations	11.8	11.4	14.9	10.2	17.0
Production occupations	5.8	5.7	5.9	6.9	8.7
Transportation and material moving occupations	5.9	5.7	9.0	3.3	8.3

See note at end of table.

17

Table 7. **Employed people by occupation, sex, race, and Hispanic or Latino ethnicity, 2011 annual averages—Continued**

Occupation and sex	Total	White	Black or African American	Asian	Hispanic or Latino ethnicity
Men, 16 years and older (thousands)	74,290	61,920	6,953	3,703	12,049
Percent	100.0	100.0	100.0	100.0	100.0
Management, professional, and related occupations	34.4	34.9	23.5	49.1	15.6
Management, business, and financial operations occupations	16.5	17.4	9.7	16.9	7.7
Management occupations	12.7	13.5	6.7	11.8	6.0
Business and financial operations occupations	3.8	3.9	3.0	5.0	1.7
Professional and related occupations	17.9	17.6	13.8	32.3	7.9
Computer and mathematical occupations	3.6	3.3	2.2	12.4	1.4
Architecture and engineering occupations	3.2	3.3	1.7	5.6	1.3
Life, physical, and social science occupations	0.9	0.9	0.7	1.7	0.4
Community and social service occupations	1.1	1.0	2.2	0.7	0.7
Legal occupations	1.2	1.3	0.6	0.9	0.3
Education, training, and library occupations	3.1	3.1	2.6	3.5	1.4
Arts, design, entertainment, sports, and media occupations	2.0	2.1	1.5	1.6	1.2
Healthcare practitioner and technical occupations	2.7	2.5	2.3	5.9	1.3
Service occupations	14.7	13.8	22.3	14.2	21.9
Healthcare support occupations	0.6	0.4	1.6	0.8	0.5
Protective service occupations	3.4	3.3	5.5	1.6	2.6
Food preparation and serving related occupations	4.8	4.4	6.7	6.7	8.1
Building and grounds cleaning and maintenance occupations	4.5	4.4	6.2	2.6	9.3
Personal care and service occupations	1.4	1.3	2.4	2.6	1.3
Sales and office occupations	16.8	16.6	18.0	17.1	14.6
Sales and related occupations	10.4	10.7	8.2	10.4	7.8
Office and administrative support occupations	6.3	5.9	9.8	6.7	6.8
Natural resources, construction, and maintenance occupations	16.8	17.9	11.6	6.5	26.1
Farming, fishing, and forestry occupations	1.1	1.2	0.5	0.2	2.8
Construction and extraction occupations	9.4	10.1	5.9	2.8	17.1
Installation, maintenance, and repair occupations	6.3	6.6	5.3	3.5	6.2
Production, transportation, and material moving occupations	17.4	16.8	24.6	13.0	21.8
Production occupations	7.8	7.8	8.1	7.8	9.8
Transportation and material moving occupations	9.5	9.0	16.5	5.3	12.0

See note at end of table.

Table 7. **Employed people by occupation, sex, race, and Hispanic or Latino ethnicity, 2011 annual averages—Continued**

Occupation and sex	Total	White	Black or African American	Asian	Hispanic or Latino ethnicity
Women, 16 years and older (thousands)	65,579	52,770	8,098	3,165	8,220
Percent	100.0	100.0	100.0	100.0	100.0
Management, professional, and related occupations	41.2	42.3	34.1	44.4	25.2
Management, business, and financial operations occupations	14.2	14.7	11.2	15.4	8.9
Management occupations	8.9	9.4	6.1	8.1	5.4
Business and financial operations occupations	5.3	5.3	5.1	7.2	3.5
Professional and related occupations	27.0	27.6	22.9	29.0	16.3
Computer and mathematical occupations	1.4	1.2	1.2	4.4	0.5
Architecture and engineering occupations	0.6	0.6	0.3	1.1	0.3
Life, physical, and social science occupations	0.9	0.9	0.6	2.1	0.4
Community and social service occupations	2.3	2.2	3.4	1.2	2.0
Legal occupations	1.3	1.4	1.1	1.1	0.8
Education, training, and library occupations	9.7	10.2	8.0	5.6	6.7
Arts, design, entertainment, sports, and media occupations	2.0	2.2	0.8	1.4	1.3
Healthcare practitioner and technical occupations	8.8	8.8	7.6	12.1	4.4
Service occupations	21.1	19.9	28.0	21.8	31.2
Healthcare support occupations	4.5	3.8	8.8	3.7	4.9
Protective service occupations	1.0	0.9	2.2	0.3	1.0
Food preparation and serving related occupations	6.4	6.4	6.3	6.6	8.7
Building and grounds cleaning and maintenance occupations	3.3	3.2	4.0	2.3	9.6
Personal care and service occupations	6.0	5.6	6.6	8.9	7.0
Sales and office occupations	31.4	31.8	30.8	26.3	31.8
Sales and related occupations	11.6	11.6	11.5	11.4	12.2
Office and administrative support occupations	19.9	20.2	19.3	14.9	19.6
Natural resources, construction, and maintenance occupations	0.8	0.9	0.5	0.6	1.8
Farming, fishing, and forestry occupations	0.3	0.4	0.1	0.2	1.1
Construction and extraction occupations	0.2	0.3	0.1	0.1	0.4
Installation, maintenance, and repair occupations	0.3	0.3	0.2	0.3	0.3
Production, transportation, and material moving occupations	5.4	5.1	6.7	6.9	10.1
Production occupations	3.5	3.3	4.1	6.0	7.1
Transportation and material moving occupations	1.9	1.8	2.6	0.9	3.0

NOTE: Estimates for the above race groups (White, Black or African American, and Asian) do not sum to totals because data are not presented for all races. People whose ethnicity is identified as Hispanic or Latino may be of any race. Effective with January 2011 data, occupations reflect the introduction of the 2010 Census occupational classification system, derived from the 2010 Standard Occupational Classification (SOC). No historical data have been revised. Data for 2011 are not strictly comparable with data for earlier years. More information about the change in classification is available online at **http://www.bls.gov/cps/documentation.htm#oi**.

Table 8. **Employed people by detailed occupation, race, and Hispanic or Latino ethnicity, 2011 annual averages**

(Numbers in thousands)

Occupation	Total employed	Percent of total employed			
		White	Black or African American	Asian	Hispanic or Latino ethnicity
Total, 16 years and over	139,869	82.0	10.8	4.9	14.5
Management, professional, and related occupations	52,547	83.6	8.4	6.1	7.5
Management, business, and financial operations occupations	21,589	85.7	7.3	5.1	7.7
Management occupations	15,250	87.3	6.3	4.6	7.7
Chief executives	1,515	92.7	2.7	3.0	4.1
General and operations managers	978	89.7	6.6	2.7	7.6
Legislators	16	–	–	–	–
Advertising and promotions managers	87	94.3	1.6	1.5	5.6
Marketing and sales managers	1,009	87.1	5.6	5.6	6.6
Public relations and fundraising managers	63	95.2	2.8	0.4	3.1
Administrative services managers	128	87.5	6.9	2.2	7.3
Computer and information systems managers	553	79.4	5.7	12.9	3.8
Financial managers	1,107	86.3	6.5	5.8	8.7
Compensation and benefits managers	21	–	–	–	–
Human resources managers	243	85.6	11.3	2.1	9.5
Training and development managers	38	–	–	–	–
Industrial production managers	259	89.6	3.9	5.1	8.9
Purchasing managers	204	85.3	8.8	2.1	8.8
Transportation, storage, and distribution managers	254	87.4	8.7	3.0	8.9
Farmers, ranchers, and other agricultural managers	978	96.2	0.9	0.8	4.1
Construction managers	926	94.1	3.0	1.5	9.7
Education administrators	853	81.7	13.3	2.9	6.5
Architectural and engineering managers	106	91.5	1.3	5.9	4.7
Food service managers	1,051	79.2	9.2	9.2	13.9
Funeral service managers	13	–	–	–	–
Gaming managers	23	–	–	–	–
Lodging managers	148	77.7	7.0	13.4	8.1
Medical and health services managers	529	80.9	11.2	5.0	8.4
Natural sciences managers	16	–	–	–	–
Postmasters and mail superintendents	40	–	–	–	–
Property, real estate, and community association managers	587	85.5	8.8	3.1	8.8
Social and community service managers	329	84.5	11.3	2.6	6.9
Emergency management directors	5	–	–	–	–
Managers, all other	3,173	86.7	5.9	5.4	8.6
Business and financial operations occupations	6,339	81.8	9.8	6.6	7.8
Agents and business managers of artists, performers, and athletes ...	48	–	–	–	–
Buyers and purchasing agents, farm products	12	–	–	–	–
Wholesale and retail buyers, except farm products	170	89.4	4.2	4.7	11.8
Purchasing agents, except wholesale, retail, and farm products	259	85.3	8.7	3.5	5.3
Claims adjusters, appraisers, examiners, and investigators	296	79.1	16.5	2.3	9.5
Compliance officers	198	82.3	10.9	3.8	9.4
Cost estimators	119	93.3	2.7	2.3	6.0
Human resources workers	595	78.5	15.1	4.4	10.5
Compensation, benefits, and job analysis specialists	65	84.6	10.7	2.3	5.2
Training and development specialists	130	79.2	13.6	4.4	8.5
Logisticians	88	88.6	7.3	1.7	12.3
Management analysts	707	83.0	6.8	8.5	4.5
Meeting, convention, and event planners	109	84.4	11.6	2.0	12.4
Fundraisers	78	91.0	3.9	3.0	3.7
Market research analysts and marketing specialists	205	85.9	5.2	7.3	6.3
Business operations specialists, all other	281	82.2	12.2	4.5	8.7
Accountants and auditors	1,653	79.5	8.5	10.3	7.6

See note at end of table.

(Levels in thousands)

Occupation	Total employed	Percent of total employed			
		White	Black or African American	Asian	Hispanic or Latino ethnicity
Appraisers and assessors of real estate	88	90.9	3.7	1.6	0.0
Budget analysts	53	69.8	20.1	8.9	3.6
Credit analysts	24	–	–	–	–
Financial analysts	84	79.8	6.0	13.4	2.7
Personal financial advisors	371	86.5	6.8	5.6	6.7
Insurance underwriters	117	84.6	10.7	3.0	3.0
Financial examiners	8	–	–	–	–
Credit counselors and loan officers	326	81.0	12.1	5.5	11.4
Tax examiners and collectors, and revenue agents	70	67.1	24.2	8.6	10.8
Tax preparers	110	81.8	9.8	5.8	11.9
Financial specialists, all other	77	68.8	16.4	11.2	7.5
Professional and related occupations	30,957	82.1	9.1	6.8	7.4
Computer and mathematical occupations	3,608	74.7	6.9	16.6	5.7
Computer and information research scientists	20	–	–	–	–
Computer systems analysts	447	76.7	7.1	14.9	4.4
Information security analysts	44	–	–	–	–
Computer programmers	459	78.0	4.3	15.4	5.8
Software developers, applications and systems software	1,044	66.9	4.8	27.1	4.6
Web developers	182	80.8	5.9	11.1	6.9
Computer support specialists	461	77.0	11.8	8.7	7.5
Database administrators	134	76.9	9.2	11.8	9.0
Network and computer systems administrators	233	82.0	6.2	10.0	7.2
Computer network architects	98	81.6	3.1	13.9	7.0
Computer occupations, all other	306	77.8	8.8	11.9	6.5
Actuaries	18	–	–	–	–
Mathematicians	2	–	–	–	–
Operations research analysts	116	76.7	14.5	6.5	4.1
Statisticians	37	–	–	–	–
Miscellaneous mathematical science occupations	6	–	–	–	–
Architecture and engineering occupations	2,785	84.5	5.2	8.8	6.4
Architects, except naval	181	90.6	1.6	5.5	4.1
Surveyors, cartographers, and photogrammetrists	42	–	–	–	–
Aerospace engineers	144	85.4	5.7	8.0	8.2
Agricultural engineers	1	–	–	–	–
Biomedical engineers	12	–	–	–	–
Chemical engineers	74	81.1	5.5	13.8	5.1
Civil engineers	383	86.9	4.3	7.8	4.7
Computer hardware engineers	77	76.6	3.1	19.1	5.2
Electrical and electronics engineers	309	80.3	4.8	12.0	7.4
Environmental engineers	45	–	–	–	–
Industrial engineers, including health and safety	174	87.9	2.3	7.0	8.6
Marine engineers and naval architects	9	–	–	–	–
Materials engineers	32	–	–	–	–
Mechanical engineers	322	81.7	5.7	12.0	3.9
Mining and geological engineers, including mining safety engineers	11	–	–	–	–
Nuclear engineers	20	–	–	–	–
Petroleum engineers	25	–	–	–	–
Engineers, all other	337	82.8	5.7	10.5	4.7
Drafters	147	93.2	2.1	3.9	8.4
Engineering technicians, except drafters	376	80.9	11.3	6.7	9.4
Surveying and mapping technicians	62	95.2	1.7	1.9	10.0

See note at end of table.

(Levels in thousands)

Occupation	Total employed	Percent of total employed			
		White	Black or African American	Asian	Hispanic or Latino ethnicity
Life, physical, and social science occupations	1,303	81.3	7.3	9.8	5.9
Agricultural and food scientists	39	–	–	–	–
Biological scientists	114	77.2	7.7	13.5	6.8
Conservation scientists and foresters	28	–	–	–	–
Medical scientists	156	68.6	5.2	25.1	7.0
Life scientists, all other	0	–	–	–	–
Astronomers and physicists	20	–	–	–	–
Atmospheric and space scientists	7	–	–	–	–
Chemists and materials scientists	88	77.3	9.5	11.5	4.6
Environmental scientists and geoscientists	98	89.8	4.9	0.6	3.0
Physical scientists, all other	152	71.1	6.7	19.9	2.9
Economists	23	–	–	–	–
Survey researchers	3	–	–	–	–
Psychologists	197	91.4	5.1	2.9	5.9
Sociologists	4	–	–	–	–
Urban and regional planners	26	–	–	–	–
Miscellaneous social scientists and related workers	60	85.0	10.7	4.4	9.4
Agricultural and food science technicians	24	–	–	–	–
Biological technicians	21	–	–	–	–
Chemical technicians	77	85.7	9.1	5.1	14.3
Geological and petroleum technicians	10	–	–	–	–
Nuclear technicians	3	–	–	–	–
Social science research assistants	3	–	–	–	–
Miscellaneous life, physical, and social science technicians	151	76.2	11.1	9.4	6.5
Community and social service occupations	2,352	76.3	18.1	2.8	10.7
Counselors	732	75.7	18.7	2.8	11.2
Social workers	769	72.6	22.8	2.4	11.2
Probation officers and correctional treatment specialists	94	69.1	22.5	0.6	13.5
Social and human service assistants	131	73.3	18.0	2.6	19.0
Miscellaneous community and social service specialists, including health educators and community health workers	83	75.9	17.6	2.9	10.9
Clergy	414	82.4	11.3	4.1	6.8
Directors, religious activities and education	44	–	–	–	–
Religious workers, all other	85	88.2	8.5	3.0	8.6
Legal occupations	1,770	87.0	7.3	3.9	5.4
Lawyers	1,085	88.9	5.3	4.2	3.2
Judicial law clerks	5	–	–	–	–
Judges, magistrates, and other judicial workers	67	85.1	11.5	1.1	8.3
Paralegals and legal assistants	404	83.9	11.0	3.0	8.3
Miscellaneous legal support workers	209	83.7	9.3	4.3	10.5
Education, training, and library occupations	8,619	84.9	9.7	3.5	8.3
Postsecondary teachers	1,355	81.3	7.3	10.1	4.8
Preschool and kindergarten teachers	707	80.6	14.5	2.8	12.7
Elementary and middle school teachers	2,848	87.0	9.8	1.6	8.0
Secondary school teachers	1,136	88.6	7.4	2.1	6.9
Special education teachers	388	87.6	8.0	1.8	6.8
Other teachers and instructors	812	85.5	8.0	3.9	7.3
Archivists, curators, and museum technicians	48	–	–	–	–
Librarians	198	85.4	10.1	2.6	3.9
Library technicians	37	–	–	–	–
Teacher assistants	950	80.4	14.3	2.6	14.9
Other education, training, and library workers	140	87.1	7.7	3.4	9.2

See note at end of table.

Table 8. **Employed people by detailed occupation, race, and Hispanic or Latino ethnicity, 2011 annual averages—Continued**

(Levels in thousands)

Occupation	Total employed	Percent of total employed			
		White	Black or African American	Asian	Hispanic or Latino ethnicity
Arts, design, entertainment, sports, and media occupations	2,779	87.9	6.0	3.6	9.1
Artists and related workers	180	91.1	3.8	3.8	2.8
Designers	766	90.6	3.6	3.2	10.5
Actors	28	–	–	–	–
Producers and directors	149	87.2	8.2	3.2	7.3
Athletes, coaches, umpires, and related workers	272	89.3	5.4	2.6	9.7
Dancers and choreographers	20	–	–	–	–
Musicians, singers, and related workers	191	80.6	15.1	1.2	6.6
Entertainers and performers, sports and related workers, all other	44	–	–	–	–
Announcers	53	86.8	8.5	1.1	24.8
News analysts, reporters and correspondents	70	82.9	9.3	5.0	11.4
Public relations specialists	158	88.0	6.3	2.7	9.8
Editors	166	90.4	4.6	3.8	3.4
Technical writers	60	88.3	4.2	4.6	4.1
Writers and authors	218	90.4	4.5	3.1	3.7
Miscellaneous media and communication workers	89	77.5	7.9	12.5	30.6
Broadcast and sound engineering technicians and radio operators	106	84.0	9.1	6.0	10.2
Photographers	148	89.9	3.5	2.8	9.6
Television, video, and motion picture camera operators and editors ...	57	82.5	8.6	5.7	4.5
Media and communication equipment workers, all other	3	–	–	–	–
Healthcare practitioners and technical occupations	7,740	80.5	10.0	7.8	6.7
Chiropractors	56	89.3	1.1	7.9	1.3
Dentists	181	86.2	1.0	11.0	5.8
Dietitians and nutritionists	102	80.4	15.2	4.5	8.4
Optometrists	28	–	–	–	–
Pharmacists	274	76.3	7.1	15.3	4.4
Physicians and surgeons	822	77.0	5.3	16.1	6.6
Physician assistants	82	87.8	9.6	2.7	10.1
Podiatrists	6	–	–	–	–
Audiologists	19	–	–	–	–
Occupational therapists	112	88.4	2.7	7.6	4.6
Physical therapists	222	85.1	5.2	8.9	5.0
Radiation therapists	14	–	–	–	–
Recreational therapists	14	–	–	–	–
Respiratory therapists	134	82.8	8.1	5.6	8.5
Speech-language pathologists	125	94.4	1.5	1.5	6.4
Exercise physiologists	2	–	–	–	–
Therapists, all other	138	87.0	8.0	3.2	6.0
Veterinarians	71	94.4	1.6	4.0	5.0
Registered nurses	2,706	80.4	10.4	7.3	5.1
Nurse anesthetists	33	–	–	–	–
Nurse midwives	5	–	–	–	–
Nurse practitioners	100	90.0	7.3	2.4	8.6
Health diagnosing and treating practitioners, all other	26	–	–	–	–
Clinical laboratory technologists and technicians	321	74.1	15.3	8.9	9.4
Dental hygienists	148	93.2	0.5	5.5	7.2
Diagnostic related technologists and technicians	342	86.0	9.0	4.0	7.2
Emergency medical technicians and paramedics	185	92.4	4.5	0.9	6.4
Health practitioner support technologists and technicians	511	76.7	15.1	5.6	11.0
Licensed practical and licensed vocational nurses	560	69.5	23.7	3.9	8.3
Medical records and health information technicians	116	77.6	10.6	9.5	19.6
Opticians, dispensing	51	88.2	9.4	1.8	4.8

See note at end of table.

Table 8. **Employed people by detailed occupation, race, and Hispanic or Latino ethnicity, 2011 annual averages—Continued**

(Levels in thousands)

Occupation	Total employed	Percent of total employed			
		White	Black or African American	Asian	Hispanic or Latino ethnicity
Miscellaneous health technologists and technicians	167	70.1	16.7	11.8	9.7
Other healthcare practitioners and technical occupations	70	84.3	9.4	5.1	5.6
Service occupations	24,787	76.8	15.4	4.9	21.0
Healthcare support occupations	3,359	68.2	24.6	4.3	13.9
Nursing, psychiatric, and home health aides	1,981	59.9	33.1	4.3	13.3
Occupational therapy assistants and aides	17	–	–	–	–
Physical therapist assistants and aides	75	82.7	10.4	3.5	9.7
Massage therapists	146	87.7	5.5	5.5	7.0
Dental assistants	307	83.4	8.3	5.1	16.3
Medical assistants	395	79.0	14.3	5.2	20.2
Medical transcriptionists	74	97.3	0.3	0.0	2.1
Pharmacy aides	48	–	–	–	–
Veterinary assistants and laboratory animal caretakers	38	–	–	–	–
Phlebotomists	119	64.7	26.7	4.9	13.7
Miscellaneous healthcare support occupations, including medical equipment preparers	158	67.1	24.3	2.8	13.3
Protective service occupations	3,210	77.2	17.4	2.1	12.6
First-line supervisors of correctional officers	42	–	–	–	–
First-line supervisors of police and detectives	107	85.0	9.3	4.0	6.7
First-line supervisors of fire fighting and prevention workers	44	–	–	–	–
First-line supervisors of protective service workers, all other	111	80.2	17.6	1.1	11.5
Firefighters	305	95.1	2.9	0.6	10.0
Fire inspectors	20	–	–	–	–
Bailiffs, correctional officers, and jailers	446	71.5	25.1	1.9	13.0
Detectives and criminal investigators	151	87.4	8.9	1.2	14.9
Fish and game wardens	6	–	–	–	–
Parking enforcement workers	7	–	–	–	–
Police and sheriff's patrol officers	668	83.8	11.5	2.0	12.7
Transit and railroad police	8	–	–	–	–
Animal control workers	6	–	–	–	–
Private detectives and investigators	92	89.1	8.3	1.2	11.5
Security guards and gaming surveillance officers	963	64.1	27.2	3.6	15.4
Crossing guards	59	76.3	19.7	0.0	5.5
Transportation security screeners	27	–	–	–	–
Lifeguards and other recreational, and all other protective service workers	146	89.7	6.2	0.3	6.3
Food preparation and serving related occupations	7,747	78.6	12.6	5.9	21.8
Chefs and head cooks	347	71.2	9.1	15.3	18.0
First-line supervisors of food preparation and serving workers	505	76.2	18.2	3.2	15.1
Cooks	1,990	73.5	17.9	5.9	30.4
Food preparation workers	784	76.5	14.4	5.7	23.0
Bartenders	392	90.6	5.1	2.1	10.1
Combined food preparation and serving workers, including fast food	326	77.6	16.3	3.7	15.4
Counter attendants, cafeteria, food concession, and coffee shop	255	84.3	9.1	3.5	16.9
Waiters and waitresses	2,059	82.7	7.8	6.6	17.1
Food servers, nonrestaurant	181	70.2	21.0	6.1	17.1
Dining room and cafeteria attendants and bartender helpers	347	81.3	9.8	4.9	31.5
Dishwashers	273	76.2	11.9	7.4	34.4
Hosts and hostesses, restaurant, lounge, and coffee shop	286	85.7	6.9	3.3	16.4
Food preparation and serving related workers, all other	4	–	–	–	–

See note at end of table.

Table 8. **Employed people by detailed occupation, race, and Hispanic or Latino ethnicity, 2011 annual averages—Continued**

(Levels in thousands)

Occupation	Total employed	Percent of total employed			
		White	Black or African American	Asian	Hispanic or Latino ethnicity
Building and grounds cleaning and maintenance occupations	5,492	80.5	13.7	3.1	34.8
First-line supervisors of housekeeping and janitorial workers	292	76.7	17.3	3.5	16.0
First-line supervisors of landscaping, lawn service, and groundskeeping workers	274	92.3	4.9	1.4	19.1
Janitors and building cleaners	2,186	77.4	16.6	3.1	30.4
Maids and housekeeping cleaners	1,419	76.4	16.5	4.5	39.9
Pest control workers	75	89.3	7.0	0.0	20.3
Grounds maintenance workers	1,247	88.5	7.1	1.8	45.2
Personal care and service occupations	4,979	75.3	14.1	7.6	14.7
First-line supervisors of gaming workers	120	80.0	3.7	9.1	8.4
First-line supervisors of personal service workers	192	74.0	9.9	13.8	11.0
Animal trainers	49	–	–	–	–
Nonfarm animal caretakers	179	95.0	2.7	1.4	11.0
Gaming services workers	113	66.4	5.6	23.3	16.4
Motion picture projectionists	8	–	–	–	–
Ushers, lobby attendants, and ticket takers	46	–	–	–	–
Miscellaneous entertainment attendants and related workers	182	78.0	13.9	3.8	11.3
Embalmers and funeral attendants	8	–	–	–	–
Morticians, undertakers, and funeral directors	23	–	–	–	–
Barbers	89	68.5	27.7	2.6	17.6
Hairdressers, hairstylists, and cosmetologists	758	82.1	11.6	4.1	12.8
Miscellaneous personal appearance workers	251	35.5	5.9	55.1	5.3
Baggage porters, bellhops, and concierges	81	66.7	20.7	9.1	28.4
Tour and travel guides	38	–	–	–	–
Childcare workers	1,231	79.1	15.0	3.4	18.1
Personal care aides	1,057	68.0	21.9	5.8	19.3
Recreation and fitness workers	390	84.4	10.5	3.4	7.2
Residential advisors	59	69.5	22.4	5.1	5.4
Personal care and service workers, all other	105	87.6	8.1	2.3	11.5
Sales and office occupations	33,066	81.9	11.3	4.4	13.2
Sales and related occupations	15,330	83.2	9.8	4.9	12.6
First-line supervisors of retail sales workers	3,217	83.7	8.8	5.4	10.9
First-line supervisors of non-retail sales workers	1,088	88.1	5.8	4.9	10.1
Cashiers	3,158	75.0	15.6	6.5	18.1
Counter and rental clerks	139	77.0	10.2	8.6	13.0
Parts salespersons	131	91.6	6.5	0.3	10.3
Retail salespersons	3,224	81.9	11.5	4.4	14.3
Advertising sales agents	254	85.8	10.8	1.6	8.8
Insurance sales agents	531	86.8	8.2	3.2	9.1
Securities, commodities, and financial services sales agents	267	87.3	4.7	6.5	5.6
Travel agents	69	88.4	5.9	5.3	9.5
Sales representatives, services, all other	503	85.7	7.6	4.6	10.9
Sales representatives, wholesale and manufacturing	1,297	92.2	2.9	3.4	7.9
Models, demonstrators, and product promoters	78	82.1	13.0	0.2	14.6
Real estate brokers and sales agents	811	90.0	4.6	4.2	8.8
Sales engineers	30	–	–	–	–
Telemarketers	108	78.7	14.9	1.2	17.4
Door-to-door sales workers, news and street vendors, and related workers	201	82.1	12.6	3.0	17.8
Sales and related workers, all other	226	84.5	8.5	3.3	10.0

See note at end of table.

Table 8. **Employed people by detailed occupation, race, and Hispanic or Latino ethnicity, 2011 annual averages—Continued**

(Levels in thousands)

Occupation	Total employed	Percent of total employed			
		White	Black or African American	Asian	Hispanic or Latino ethnicity
Office and administrative support occupations	17,736	80.8	12.6	4.1	13.7
First-line supervisors of office and administrative support workers	1,423	85.0	9.6	3.7	11.7
Switchboard operators, including answering service	39	–	–	–	–
Telephone operators	40	–	–	–	–
Communications equipment operators, all other	7	–	–	–	–
Bill and account collectors	211	74.4	17.3	3.8	18.4
Billing and posting clerks	471	80.5	12.3	4.5	15.2
Bookkeeping, accounting, and auditing clerks	1,300	86.3	7.7	4.1	8.4
Gaming cage workers	5	–	–	–	–
Payroll and timekeeping clerks	168	80.4	14.2	3.7	12.0
Procurement clerks	26	–	–	–	–
Tellers	413	85.2	8.7	3.9	14.8
Financial clerks, all other	64	75.0	10.4	14.1	14.9
Brokerage clerks	11	–	–	–	–
Correspondence clerks	12	–	–	–	–
Court, municipal, and license clerks	86	79.1	16.6	3.5	7.3
Credit authorizers, checkers, and clerks	45	–	–	–	–
Customer service representatives	1,916	77.3	15.7	4.5	16.9
Elig bility interviewers, government programs	85	67.1	22.4	3.3	19.7
File clerks	334	76.6	13.7	6.4	15.3
Hotel, motel, and resort desk clerks	135	67.4	19.6	7.8	16.9
Interviewers, except eligibility and loan	153	75.2	17.2	4.5	18.3
Library assistants, clerical	113	84.1	8.6	5.2	8.5
Loan interviewers and clerks	117	82.9	11.9	4.2	10.4
New accounts clerks	33	–	–	–	–
Order clerks	113	87.6	5.9	5.4	11.5
Human resources assistants, except payroll and timekeeping	40	–	–	–	–
Receptionists and information clerks	1,259	82.1	11.3	3.9	17.0
Reservation and transportation ticket agents and travel clerks	99	67.7	23.2	5.8	8.8
Information and record clerks, all other	118	79.7	15.2	2.1	11.5
Cargo and freight agents	8	–	–	–	–
Couriers and messengers	249	78.3	16.7	2.5	14.4
Dispatchers	239	78.2	17.8	1.9	12.0
Meter readers, utilities	28	–	–	–	–
Postal service clerks	146	60.3	26.4	10.9	10.1
Postal service mail carriers	348	76.7	13.7	6.9	10.0
Postal service mail sorters, processors, and processing machine operators	60	60.0	30.5	8.9	16.2
Production, planning, and expediting clerks	236	85.6	8.9	2.9	9.5
Shipping, receiving, and traffic clerks	559	78.9	14.2	3.7	24.3
Stock clerks and order fillers	1,503	78.2	15.5	3.4	18.8
Weighers, measurers, checkers, and samplers, recordkeeping	70	77.1	17.6	5.0	22.1
Secretaries and administrative assistants	2,871	86.8	8.2	2.6	9.7
Computer operators	126	81.0	11.1	5.9	11.1
Data entry keyers	334	76.0	16.0	4.9	12.6
Word processors and typists	136	73.5	18.8	6.2	10.0
Desktop publishers	2	–	–	–	–
Insurance claims and policy processing clerks	246	78.0	17.4	2.1	10.1
Mail clerks and mail machine operators, except postal service	93	76.3	18.0	3.3	15.0
Office clerks, general	1,061	78.1	13.5	5.0	15.5
Office machine operators, except computer	45	–	–	–	–
Proofreaders and copy markers	7	–	–	–	–

See note at end of table.

26

Table 8. **Employed people by detailed occupation, race, and Hispanic or Latino ethnicity, 2011 annual averages—Continued**

(Levels in thousands)

Occupation	Total employed	Percent of total employed			
		White	Black or African American	Asian	Hispanic or Latino ethnicity
Statistical assistants	18	–	–	–	–
Office and administrative support workers, all other	513	79.5	14.2	4.0	12.6
Natural resources, construction, and maintenance occupations	13,009	88.9	6.5	2.0	25.3
Farming, fishing, and forestry occupations	1,001	91.8	4.3	1.4	43.0
First-line supervisors of farming, fishing, and forestry workers	52	96.2	1.0	0.0	23.2
Agricultural inspectors	22	–	–	–	–
Animal breeders	10	–	–	–	–
Graders and sorters, agricultural products	95	83.2	12.6	3.6	51.5
Miscellaneous agricultural workers	708	93.6	2.8	1.3	49.6
Fishers and related fishing workers	37	–	–	–	–
Hunters and trappers	2	–	–	–	–
Forest and conservation workers	14	–	–	–	–
Logging workers	61	90.2	7.0	0.0	9.1
Construction and extraction occupations	7,125	90.1	5.9	1.5	29.4
First-line supervisors of construction trades and extraction workers	634	93.2	5.2	0.7	16.5
Boilermakers	19	–	–	–	–
Brickmasons, blockmasons, and stonemasons	146	89.0	5.0	1.9	39.3
Carpenters	1,330	90.6	5.3	1.6	26.7
Carpet, floor, and tile installers and finishers	189	88.9	6.3	2.4	43.2
Cement masons, concrete finishers, and terrazzo workers	70	88.6	9.3	0.6	47.8
Construction laborers	1,253	88.4	7.3	1.8	42.9
Paving, surfacing, and tamping equipment operators	21	–	–	–	–
Pile-driver operators	1	–	–	–	–
Operating engineers and other construction equipment operators	369	90.8	5.0	0.2	16.6
Drywall installers, ceiling tile installers, and tapers	150	90.7	2.0	0.6	59.7
Electricians	682	89.6	6.1	2.4	14.0
Glaziers	48	–	–	–	–
Insulation workers	47	–	–	–	–
Painters, construction and maintenance	528	88.4	6.5	2.5	41.8
Paperhangers	8	–	–	–	–
Pipelayers, plumbers, pipefitters, and steamfitters	519	89.8	6.4	1.4	22.5
Plasterers and stucco masons	24	–	–	–	–
Reinforcing iron and rebar workers	7	–	–	–	–
Roofers	222	92.3	4.9	0.8	47.3
Sheet metal workers	126	93.7	2.2	0.6	18.9
Structural iron and steel workers	66	93.9	4.1	0.0	19.5
Solar photovoltaic installers	5	–	–	–	–
Helpers, construction trades	63	82.5	10.5	2.4	41.1
Construction and building inspectors	75	90.7	5.0	0.2	11.6
Elevator installers and repairers	30	–	–	–	–
Fence erectors	45	–	–	–	–
Hazardous materials removal workers	32	–	–	–	–
Highway maintenance workers	105	86.7	11.0	0.5	13.2
Rail-track laying and maintenance equipment operators	7	–	–	–	–
Septic tank servicers and sewer pipe cleaners	11	–	–	–	–
Miscellaneous construction and related workers	36	–	–	–	–
Derrick, rotary drill, and service unit operators, oil, gas, and mining	46	–	–	–	–
Earth drillers, except oil and gas	23	–	–	–	–
Explosives workers, ordnance handling experts, and blasters	9	–	–	–	–
Mining machine operators	78	93.6	3.0	0.0	15.5

See note at end of table.

(Levels in thousands)

Occupation	Total employed	Percent of total employed			
		White	Black or African American	Asian	Hispanic or Latino ethnicity
Roof bolters, mining	10	–	–	–	–
Roustabouts, oil and gas	17	–	–	–	–
Helpers--extraction workers	8	–	–	–	–
Other extraction workers	68	95.6	1.1	1.9	36.1
Installation, maintenance, and repair occupations	4,883	86.7	7.9	2.9	15.8
First-line supervisors of mechanics, installers, and repairers	313	90.4	6.4	0.9	9.7
Computer, automated teller, and office machine repairers	305	81.3	11.0	6.3	9.9
Radio and telecommunications equipment installers and repairers	150	83.3	10.1	3.2	10.6
Avionics technicians	16	–	–	–	–
Electric motor, power tool, and related repairers	35	–	–	–	–
Electrical and electronics installers and repairers, transportation equipment	6	–	–	–	–
Electrical and electronics repairers, industrial and utility	14	–	–	–	–
Electronic equipment installers and repairers, motor vehicles	20	–	–	–	–
Electronic home entertainment equipment installers and repairers	38	–	–	–	–
Security and fire alarm systems installers	53	88.7	6.3	1.0	17.8
Aircraft mechanics and service technicians	164	85.4	8.9	3.1	17.2
Automotive body and related repairers	140	90.0	6.9	2.9	18.1
Automotive glass installers and repairers	17	–	–	–	–
Automotive service technicians and mechanics	855	84.9	7.8	4.2	19.7
Bus and truck mechanics and diesel engine specialists	312	90.4	4.0	2.5	15.1
Heavy vehicle and mobile equipment service technicians and mechanics	199	92.0	5.0	1.2	11.1
Small engine mechanics	52	90.4	6.4	0.1	8.6
Miscellaneous vehicle and mobile equipment mechanics, installers, and repairers	95	90.5	6.3	0.1	21.0
Control and valve installers and repairers	24	–	–	–	–
Heating, air conditioning, and refrigeration mechanics and installers	338	90.8	5.8	1.9	16.9
Home appliance repairers	43	–	–	–	–
Industrial and refractory machinery mechanics	433	86.6	7.1	3.8	15.2
Maintenance and repair workers, general	422	83.6	12.2	1.9	17.4
Maintenance workers, machinery	38	–	–	–	–
Millwrights	58	93.1	4.7	0.8	3.0
Electrical power-line installers and repairers	124	89.5	8.6	0.4	11.5
Telecommunications line installers and repairers	201	83.1	12.2	1.1	17.3
Precision instrument and equipment repairers	76	90.8	5.0	2.7	21.6
Wind turbine service technicians	2	–	–	–	–
Coin, vending, and amusement machine servicers and repairers	46	–	–	–	–
Commercial divers	0	–	–	–	–
Locksmiths and safe repairers	28	–	–	–	–
Manufactured building and mobile home installers	7	–	–	–	–
Riggers	14	–	–	–	–
Signal and track switch repairers	5	–	–	–	–
Helpers--installation, maintenance, and repair workers	24	–	–	–	–
Other installation, maintenance, and repair workers	215	85.6	9.2	3.0	23.3
Production, transportation, and material moving occupations	16,461	79.5	13.7	4.3	21.0
Production occupations	8,142	80.8	11.0	5.9	21.6
First-line supervisors of production and operating workers	727	85.1	7.7	5.6	12.7
Aircraft structure, surfaces, rigging, and systems assemblers	20	–	–	–	–
Electrical, electronics, and electromechanical assemblers	156	64.7	13.5	21.5	20.4

See note at end of table.

Table 8. **Employed people by detailed occupation, race, and Hispanic or Latino ethnicity, 2011 annual averages—Continued**

(Levels in thousands)

Occupation	Total employed	Percent of total employed			
		White	Black or African American	Asian	Hispanic or Latino ethnicity
Engine and other machine assemblers	34	–	–	–	–
Structural metal fabricators and fitters	32	–	–	–	–
Miscellaneous assemblers and fabricators	860	73.7	16.3	7.5	20.3
Bakers	207	80.7	13.3	5.0	32.9
Butchers and other meat, poultry, and fish processing workers	342	70.5	17.2	10.6	38.0
Food and tobacco roasting, baking, and drying machine operators and tenders	12	–	–	–	–
Food batchmakers	90	78.9	15.3	4.3	29.3
Food cooking machine operators and tenders	24	–	–	–	–
Food processing workers, all other	115	79.1	14.2	2.5	39.8
Computer control programmers and operators	72	88.9	4.5	6.0	12.9
Extruding and drawing machine setters, operators, and tenders, metal and plastic	13	–	–	–	–
Forging machine setters, operators, and tenders, metal and plastic	6	–	–	–	–
Rolling machine setters, operators, and tenders, metal and plastic	8	–	–	–	–
Cutting, punching, and press machine setters, operators, and tenders, metal and plastic	100	83.0	10.7	3.3	18.2
Drilling and boring machine tool setters, operators, and tenders, metal and plastic	5	–	–	–	–
Grinding, lapping, polishing, and buffing machine tool setters, operators, and tenders, metal and plastic	65	86.2	10.0	0.2	29.6
Lathe and turning machine tool setters, operators, and tenders, metal and plastic	15	–	–	–	–
Milling and planing machine setters, operators, and tenders metal and plastic	4	–	–	–	–
Machinists	419	89.5	3.7	4.2	14.1
Metal furnace operators, tenders, pourers, and casters	16	–	–	–	–
Model makers and patternmakers, metal and plastic	7	–	–	–	–
Molders and molding machine setters, operators, and tenders, metal and plastic	45	–	–	–	–
Multiple machine tool setters, operators, and tenders, metal and plastic	5	–	–	–	–
Tool and die makers	66	93.9	3.7	0.6	9.4
Welding, soldering, and brazing workers	505	86.7	7.6	3.8	20.9
Heat treating equipment setters, operators, and tenders, metal and plastic	4	–	–	–	–
Layout workers, metal and plastic	6	–	–	–	–
Plating and coating machine setters, operators, and tenders, metal and plastic	15	–	–	–	–
Tool grinders, filers, and sharpeners	7	–	–	–	–
Metal workers and plastic workers, all other	368	79.6	10.3	7.2	24.3
Prepress technicians and workers	41	–	–	–	–
Printing press operators	217	83.4	12.0	2.2	16.9
Print binding and finishing workers	16	–	–	–	–
Laundry and dry-cleaning workers	174	70.7	15.2	10.4	33.8
Pressers, textile, garment, and related materials	48	–	–	–	–
Sewing machine operators	169	76.9	9.7	12.0	36.9
Shoe and leather workers and repairers	11	–	–	–	–
Shoe machine operators and tenders	8	–	–	–	–
Tailors, dressmakers, and sewers	94	81.9	4.2	10.7	27.5
Textile bleaching and dyeing machine operators and tenders	1	–	–	–	–
Textile cutting machine setters, operators, and tenders	5	–	–	–	–
Textile knitting and weaving machine setters, operators, and tenders	14	–	–	–	–

See note at end of table.

Table 8. Employed people by detailed occupation, race, and Hispanic or Latino ethnicity, 2011 annual averages—Continued

(Levels in thousands)

Occupation	Total employed	Percent of total employed			
		White	Black or African American	Asian	Hispanic or Latino ethnicity
Textile winding, twisting, and drawing out machine setters, operators, and tenders	16	–	–	–	–
Extruding and forming machine setters, operators, and tenders, synthetic and glass fibers	1	–	–	–	–
Fabric and apparel patternmakers	5	–	–	–	–
Upholsterers	47	–	–	–	–
Textile, apparel, and furnishings workers, all other	22	–	–	–	–
Cabinetmakers and bench carpenters	66	95.5	0.3	1.5	8.0
Furniture finishers	17	–	–	–	–
Model makers and patternmakers, wood	1	–	–	–	–
Sawing machine setters, operators, and tenders, wood	32	–	–	–	–
Woodworking machine setters, operators, and tenders, except sawing	20	–	–	–	–
Woodworkers, all other	21	–	–	–	–
Power plant operators, distributors, and dispatchers	50	88.0	5.9	2.0	6.5
Stationary engineers and boiler operators	95	83.2	13.5	3.4	17.4
Water and wastewater treatment plant and system operators	71	83.1	11.1	0.8	10.8
Miscellaneous plant and system operators	39	–	–	–	–
Chemical processing machine setters, operators, and tenders	65	86.2	9.8	2.4	11.3
Crushing, grinding, polishing, mixing, and blending workers	94	86.2	8.1	3.9	21.0
Cutting workers	84	85.7	9.8	1.2	28.5
Extruding, forming, pressing, and compacting machine setters, operators, and tenders	34	–	–	–	–
Furnace, kiln, oven, drier, and kettle operators and tenders	11	–	–	–	–
Inspectors, testers, sorters, samplers, and weighers	647	82.7	8.1	6.0	16.4
Jewelers and precious stone and metal workers	41	–	–	–	–
Medical, dental, and ophthalmic laboratory technicians	87	81.6	7.3	9.8	13.0
Packaging and filling machine operators and tenders	288	78.1	13.3	5.6	40.9
Painting workers	120	83.3	10.8	3.1	23.1
Photographic process workers and processing machine operators	43	–	–	–	–
Semiconductor processors	3	–	–	–	–
Adhesive bonding machine operators and tenders	9	–	–	–	–
Cleaning, washing, and metal pickling equipment operators and tenders	11	–	–	–	–
Cooling and freezing equipment operators and tenders	3	–	–	–	–
Etchers and engravers	10	–	–	–	–
Molders, shapers, and casters, except metal and plastic	37	–	–	–	–
Paper goods machine setters, operators, and tenders	37	–	–	–	–
Tire builders	20	–	–	–	–
Helpers--production workers	54	85.2	11.2	3.4	30.6
Production workers, all other	777	77.7	14.7	5.3	21.5
Transportation and material moving occupations	8,318	78.3	16.3	2.7	20.3
Supervisors of transportation and material moving workers	228	78.1	16.5	2.3	13.7
Aircraft pilots and flight engineers	121	94.2	2.9	2.4	3.9
Air traffic controllers and airfield operations specialists	43	–	–	–	–
Flight attendants	88	86.4	9.3	3.2	10.4
Ambulance drivers and attendants, except emergency medical technicians	13	–	–	–	–
Bus drivers	573	70.5	24.6	1.6	12.7
Driver/sales workers and truck drivers	3,059	82.7	13.7	1.6	17.6
Taxi drivers and chauffeurs	342	54.4	26.7	15.6	16.0
Motor vehicle operators, all other	62	82.3	13.5	3.4	21.2
Locomotive engineers and operators	45	–	–	–	–

See note at end of table.

(Levels in thousands)

Occupation	Total employed	Percent of total employed			
		White	Black or African American	Asian	Hispanic or Latino ethnicity
Railroad brake, signal, and switch operators	5	–	–	–	–
Railroad conductors and yardmasters	52	67.3	27.2	2.7	4.7
Subway, streetcar, and other rail transportation workers	11	–	–	–	–
Sailors and marine oilers	22	–	–	–	–
Ship and boat captains and operators	37	–	–	–	–
Ship engineers	8	–	–	–	–
Bridge and lock tenders	6	–	–	–	–
Parking lot attendants	73	61.6	26.6	4.1	28.7
Automotive and watercraft service attendants	76	84.2	7.1	2.3	17.1
Transportation inspectors	32	–	–	–	–
Transportation attendants, except flight attendants	32	–	–	–	–
Other transportation workers	16	–	–	–	–
Conveyor operators and tenders	5	–	–	–	–
Crane and tower operators	63	82.5	13.7	1.9	21.8
Dredge, excavating, and loading machine operators	51	94.1	0.0	0.0	17.2
Hoist and winch operators	4	–	–	–	–
Industrial truck and tractor operators	528	73.7	22.7	1.3	27.9
Cleaners of vehicles and equipment	331	80.7	14.2	1.3	33.4
Laborers and freight, stock, and material movers, hand	1,787	76.7	17.4	3.1	21.8
Machine feeders and offbearers	36	–	–	–	–
Packers and packagers, hand	393	78.6	14.1	3.6	45.8
Pumping station operators	21	–	–	–	–
Refuse and recyclable material collectors	92	75.0	17.1	0.7	30.0
Mine shuttle car operators	1	–	–	–	–
Tank car, truck, and ship loaders	3	–	–	–	–
Material moving workers, all other	62	80.6	16.4	0.4	24.0

NOTE: Estimates for the above race groups (White, Black or African American, and Asian) do not sum to totals because data are not presented for all races. People whose ethnicity is identified as Hispanic or Latino may be of any race. Dash indicates no data or data that do not meet publication criteria (values not shown where base is less than 50,000). Effective with January 2011 data, occupations reflect the introduction of the 2010 Census occupational classification system, derived from the 2010 Standard Occupational Classification (SOC). No historical data have been revised. Data for 2011 are not strictly comparable with data for earlier years. More information about the change in classification is available online at **http://www.bls.gov/cps/documentation.htm#oi.**

Table 9. **Employed people by industry, sex, race, and Hispanic or Latino ethnicity, 2011 annual averages**

Industry and sex	Total	White	Black or African American	Asian	Hispanic or Latino ethnicity
Total, 16 years and older (thousands)	139,869	114,690	15,051	6,867	20,269
Percent	100.0	100.0	100.0	100.0	100.0
Agriculture and related industries	1.6	1.9	0.3	0.3	2.6
Mining, quarrying, and oil and gas extraction	0.6	0.6	0.2	0.2	0.6
Construction	6.5	7.2	3.3	2.0	10.9
Manufacturing	10.2	10.4	8.3	12.6	10.6
Durable goods	6.4	6.6	4.3	8.6	5.6
Nondurable goods	3.8	3.8	3.9	4.0	5.0
Wholesale and retail trade	14.1	14.3	13.3	13.0	14.4
Wholesale trade	2.7	2.8	1.9	2.5	2.9
Retail trade	11.4	11.4	11.4	10.5	11.5
Transportation and utilities	5.1	4.9	7.5	4.1	5.4
Information	2.3	2.2	2.3	2.6	1.5
Financial activities	6.7	6.8	5.9	7.6	4.9
Professional and business services	11.3	11.5	9.1	14.1	11.5
Education and health services	22.8	22.0	29.3	22.2	16.5
Leisure and hospitality	9.1	8.8	9.5	11.8	12.3
Other services	4.8	4.8	4.1	6.4	5.5
Other services, except private households	4.3	4.3	3.7	6.0	4.2
Private households	0.5	0.5	0.4	0.4	1.3
Public administration	4.9	4.7	7.0	3.2	3.4
Men, 16 years and older (thousands)	74,290	61,920	6,953	3,703	12,049
Percent	100.0	100.0	100.0	100.0	100.0
Agriculture and related industries	2.3	2.6	0.7	0.4	3.5
Mining, quarrying, and oil and gas extraction	1.0	1.1	0.5	0.3	1.0
Construction	11.1	12.0	6.6	3.3	17.5
Manufacturing	13.8	14.0	11.8	15.2	12.4
Durable goods	9.1	9.4	6.4	10.8	7.1
Nondurable goods	4.6	4.6	5.4	4.4	5.4
Wholesale and retail trade	14.7	14.7	15.0	13.3	14.0
Wholesale trade	3.7	3.8	3.1	2.9	3.6
Retail trade	11.0	11.0	11.9	10.3	10.4
Transportation and utilities	7.5	7.1	11.8	5.7	7.4
Information	2.5	2.5	2.5	3.3	1.6
Financial activities	5.7	5.8	4.8	7.0	3.7
Professional and business services	12.6	12.5	10.6	17.3	12.2
Education and health services	11.0	10.3	14.8	14.3	7.0
Leisure and hospitality	8.5	8.0	10.1	12.1	11.7
Other services	4.3	4.3	4.4	4.9	4.7
Other services, except private households	4.2	4.2	4.3	4.8	4.5
Private households	0.1	0.1	0.1	0.1	0.2
Public administration	5.1	5.0	6.4	3.0	3.2

See note at end of table.

Table 9. **Employed people by industry, sex, race, and Hispanic or Latino ethnicity, 2011 annual averages—Continued**

Industry and sex	Total	White	Black or African American	Asian	Hispanic or Latino ethnicity
Women, 16 years and older (thousands)	65,579	52,770	8,098	3,165	8,220
Percent	100.0	100.0	100.0	100.0	100.0
Agriculture and related industries	0.8	1.0	0.1	0.3	1.3
Mining, quarrying, and oil and gas extraction	0.2	0.2	0.1	0.1	0.1
Construction	1.3	1.4	0.5	0.4	1.1
Manufacturing	6.3	6.2	5.2	9.5	7.9
Durable goods	3.4	3.4	2.6	5.9	3.5
Nondurable goods	2.9	2.9	2.7	3.6	4.4
Wholesale and retail trade	13.5	13.8	11.9	12.7	14.9
Wholesale trade	1.7	1.8	0.9	2.1	1.9
Retail trade	11.8	12.0	11.0	10.6	13.0
Transportation and utilities	2.5	2.3	3.8	2.1	2.5
Information	1.9	1.9	2.1	1.7	1.3
Financial activities	7.8	8.0	6.7	8.2	6.7
Professional and business services	9.9	10.2	7.8	10.5	10.3
Education and health services	36.1	35.6	41.7	31.4	30.4
Leisure and hospitality	9.8	9.7	8.9	11.5	13.2
Other services	5.3	5.4	3.8	8.2	6.7
Other services, except private households	4.3	4.3	3.2	7.5	3.8
Private households	1.0	1.0	0.7	0.7	2.8
Public administration	4.7	4.3	7.4	3.3	3.7

NOTE: Estimates for the above race groups (White, Black or African American, and Asian) do not sum to totals because data are not presented for all races. People whose ethnicity is identified as Hispanic or Latino may be of any race.

Table 10. **Employment and unemployment in families by type of family, race, and Hispanic or Latino ethnicity, 2011 annual averages**

(Numbers in thousands)

Family type and employment status of family members	Total	White	Black or African American	Asian	Hispanic or Latino ethnicity
Total families	78,362	63,635	9,370	3,559	10,902
With at least one family member employed	62,529	51,030	6,954	3,131	9,178
As a percent of total families	79.8	80.2	74.2	88.0	84.2
With at least one family member unemployed	9,043	6,608	1,767	389	1,781
As a percent of total families	11.5	10.4	18.9	10.9	16.3
Some family member(s) employed	6,079	4,627	985	298	1,226
As a percent of families with at least one member unemployed	67.2	70.0	55.7	76.4	68.8
Some family member(s) employed full time	5,211	3,964	835	270	1,030
As a percent of families with at least one member unemployed	57.6	60.0	47.3	69.4	57.8
Married-couple families	57,920	49,164	4,193	2,861	6,805
With at least one family member employed	46,910	39,997	3,444	2,557	6,043
As a percent of total families	81.9	81.4	82.1	89.4	88.8
With at least one family member unemployed	5,576	4,448	691	294	1,071
As a percent of total families	9.6	9.0	16.5	10.3	15.7
Some family member(s) employed	4,413	3,529	533	242	852
As a percent of families with at least one member unemployed	79.2	79.3	77.2	82.3	79.5
Some family member(s) employed full time	3,861	3,070	473	222	722
As a percent of families with at least one member unemployed	69.2	69.0	68.5	75.5	67.4
Families maintained by women	15,147	9,973	4,219	438	2,723
With at least one family member employed	10,867	7,344	2,824	352	1,955
As a percent of total families	71.7	73.6	66.9	80.5	71.8
With at least one family member unemployed	2,498	1,470	875	55	478
As a percent of total families	16.5	14.7	20.7	12.6	17.6
Some family member(s) employed	1,146	716	356	32	236
As a percent of families with at least one member unemployed	45.9	48.7	40.6	57.8	49.4
Some family member(s) employed full time	908	571	279	27	188
As a percent of families with at least one member unemployed	36.3	38.8	31.9	49.1	39.3
Families maintained by men	5,926	4,498	958	260	1,374
With at least one family member employed	4,752	3,689	685	222	1,180
As a percent of total families	80.2	82.0	71.6	85.4	85.9
With at least one family member unemployed	970	690	201	41	232
As a percent of total families	16.4	15.3	21.0	15.8	16.9
Some family member(s) employed	520	382	96	24	139
As a percent of families with at least one member unemployed	53.6	55.3	47.9	59.1	59.8
Some family member(s) employed full time	443	324	83	21	120
As a percent of families with at least one member unemployed	45.7	47.0	41.3	51.2	51.7

NOTE: Estimates for the above race groups (White, Black or African American, and Asian) do not sum to totals because data are not presented for all races. People whose ethnicity is identified as Hispanic or Latino may be of any race.

Table 11. **Labor force participation rates by presence and age of youngest child, sex, race, and Hispanic or Latino ethnicity, 1994–2011 annual averages**

(Percent)

Year	Total			White			Black or African American		
	Total	Men	Women	Total	Men	Women	Total	Men	Women
With no children under 18 years									
1994............	60.2	67.1	53.6	60.6	67.7	53.8	57.2	62.0	52.4
1995............	60.2	67.0	53.5	60.5	67.6	53.6	57.5	62.3	52.7
1996............	60.1	66.8	53.5	60.5	67.6	53.6	56.9	61.5	52.3
1997............	60.4	67.0	53.8	60.8	67.8	53.8	57.3	61.2	53.5
1998............	60.3	67.0	53.9	60.6	67.6	53.8	58.0	62.0	54.2
1999............	60.4	66.8	54.1	60.7	67.5	53.9	58.3	62.1	54.6
2000............	60.6	67.0	54.3	60.9	67.7	54.3	58.4	62.5	54.5
2001............	60.4	66.7	54.3	60.8	67.4	54.3	57.9	61.7	54.4
2002............	60.0	66.2	53.9	60.4	66.8	54.0	56.8	61.0	52.7
2003............	59.7	65.4	54.1	60.1	66.1	54.1	56.5	60.0	53.2
2004............	59.6	65.3	54.0	60.0	66.1	54.0	56.4	59.5	53.5
2005............	59.8	65.5	54.2	60.1	66.2	54.1	57.3	60.8	53.9
2006............	60.0	65.8	54.2	60.4	66.5	54.2	57.1	60.5	53.9
2007............	59.8	65.6	54.0	60.3	66.4	54.1	56.5	60.1	53.0
2008............	59.9	65.6	54.3	60.3	66.3	54.3	56.9	60.4	53.6
2009............	59.3	64.6	54.0	59.9	65.4	54.3	55.9	59.3	52.7
2010............	58.7	63.8	53.6	59.1	64.5	53.7	56.0	59.1	52.9
2011............	58.1	63.1	53.0	58.6	63.8	53.2	55.1	58.4	51.8
With children under 18 years									
1994............	79.8	94.1	69.0	80.9	94.8	69.5	74.9	89.5	68.4
1995............	80.3	94.1	69.8	81.3	94.9	70.3	76.3	89.6	70.3
1996............	81.1	94.5	70.8	81.8	95.3	70.7	78.5	89.7	73.3
1997............	81.8	94.6	71.9	82.4	95.4	71.7	79.6	89.6	75.0
1998............	81.8	94.6	71.8	82.2	95.3	71.3	81.0	90.4	76.7
1999............	82.0	94.6	72.2	82.3	95.4	71.5	82.0	89.3	78.5
2000............	82.1	94.7	72.3	82.3	95.3	71.6	82.2	90.3	78.2
2001............	81.9	94.6	72.1	82.2	95.3	71.5	81.8	89.7	77.9
2002............	81.6	94.3	71.8	81.9	94.8	71.1	81.9	90.3	77.7
2003............	81.2	94.1	71.1	81.4	94.7	70.3	81.5	89.7	77.5
2004............	80.7	94.1	70.4	81.1	94.8	69.8	80.5	88.4	76.5
2005............	80.7	94.1	70.5	81.1	94.8	69.8	80.4	88.7	76.3
2006............	81.0	94.1	70.9	81.4	94.9	70.2	80.5	88.1	76.9
2007............	81.4	94.3	71.0	81.7	95.0	70.3	81.2	89.6	76.6
2008............	81.5	94.1	71.4	81.8	94.8	70.8	81.1	89.7	76.7
2009............	81.3	93.8	71.4	81.8	94.5	70.9	80.2	87.7	76.3
2010............	80.9	93.7	70.8	81.4	94.5	70.5	79.7	89.0	74.9
2011............	80.6	93.5	70.6	81.1	94.3	70.2	79.6	87.9	75.3

See note at end of table.

Table 11. **Labor force participation rates by presence and age of youngest child, sex, race, and Hispanic or Latino ethnicity, 1994–2011 annual averages—Continued**

(Percent)

Year	Total			White			Black or African American		
	Total	Men	Women	Total	Men	Women	Total	Men	Women
With children 6 to 17 years, none younger									
1994.............	83.5	93.1	76.1	84.3	93.9	76.5	79.6	88.0	75.5
1995.............	83.7	93.0	76.6	84.6	93.7	77.2	80.1	88.1	76.4
1996.............	84.5	93.5	77.5	85.3	94.4	77.7	81.3	87.9	78.1
1997.............	84.7	93.6	77.9	85.4	94.4	78.0	81.8	88.1	78.7
1998.............	84.5	93.5	77.6	84.9	94.2	77.3	83.1	88.2	80.6
1999.............	84.8	93.4	78.2	85.4	94.4	78.1	83.2	86.7	81.4
2000.............	85.1	93.5	78.7	85.7	94.3	78.6	83.3	87.8	81.0
2001.............	85.0	93.6	78.3	85.5	94.5	78.1	83.3	87.5	81.1
2002.............	84.8	93.3	78.2	85.1	94.0	77.8	84.3	89.2	81.8
2003.............	84.5	93.1	77.8	84.7	93.7	77.3	84.0	88.0	82.1
2004.............	84.1	93.1	77.3	84.5	93.9	76.9	82.7	86.3	80.9
2005.............	83.7	93.0	76.5	84.1	93.8	76.3	82.4	86.9	80.2
2006.............	83.8	93.1	76.7	84.3	94.0	76.3	82.4	85.7	80.8
2007.............	84.3	93.2	77.2	84.6	94.0	76.7	83.7	87.7	81.5
2008.............	84.3	93.1	77.3	84.7	93.9	77.0	83.1	87.8	80.6
2009.............	84.2	92.7	77.3	84.7	93.7	77.0	82.2	85.7	80.3
2010.............	83.7	92.8	76.5	84.2	93.6	76.3	81.9	87.1	79.2
2011.............	83.3	92.6	76.1	83.9	93.5	76.0	81.5	86.5	78.8
With children under 6 years									
1994.............	75.8	95.2	61.2	77.1	95.9	61.6	70.0	91.3	61.2
1995.............	76.6	95.5	62.3	77.7	96.1	62.6	72.0	91.4	63.9
1996.............	77.2	95.6	63.2	77.9	96.3	62.7	75.4	91.9	68.2
1997.............	78.3	95.8	64.8	78.8	96.5	64.1	77.1	91.3	70.8
1998.............	78.6	96.1	64.9	78.9	96.6	64.1	78.5	93.0	72.0
1999.............	78.5	96.1	64.8	78.5	96.7	63.4	80.6	92.5	74.9
2000.............	78.4	96.1	64.6	78.2	96.5	63.0	80.9	93.3	74.9
2001.............	78.1	95.8	64.3	78.1	96.2	63.0	80.0	92.5	73.9
2002.............	77.7	95.5	63.7	77.9	95.9	62.7	78.9	91.8	72.5
2003.............	77.2	95.4	62.8	77.3	96.0	61.5	78.2	92.1	71.8
2004.............	76.5	95.4	61.8	76.8	96.0	60.7	77.6	91.1	70.8
2005.............	77.0	95.4	62.8	77.2	96.1	61.6	77.8	91.2	71.4
2006.............	77.5	95.4	63.5	77.7	95.9	62.5	78.0	91.1	71.8
2007.............	77.8	95.7	63.3	77.9	96.2	62.3	77.9	92.3	70.4
2008.............	77.9	95.4	64.0	78.0	95.9	62.9	78.6	92.4	71.7
2009.............	77.8	95.1	64.2	78.1	95.6	63.3	77.7	90.4	71.4
2010.............	77.5	94.7	63.9	78.0	95.5	63.4	77.1	91.3	69.8
2011.............	77.4	94.5	63.9	77.7	95.2	63.0	77.4	89.7	71.1

See note at end of table.

Table 11. **Labor force participation rates by presence and age of youngest child, sex, race, and Hispanic or Latino ethnicity, 1994–2011 annual averages—Continued**

(Percent)

Year	Total			White			Black or African American		
	Total	Men	Women	Total	Men	Women	Total	Men	Women
	With children under 3 years								
1994...........	74.0	95.3	57.7	75.6	96.0	58.6	66.0	91.5	55.6
1995...........	74.8	95.5	58.9	76.0	96.2	59.2	68.9	90.9	60.0
1996...........	75.4	95.8	59.4	76.2	96.5	59.2	72.1	92.2	63.1
1997...........	76.6	95.9	61.4	77.5	96.5	61.4	73.6	92.1	65.1
1998...........	77.2	96.2	61.9	77.7	96.7	61.5	75.8	93.2	67.5
1999...........	77.0	96.4	61.5	77.0	97.0	60.1	78.7	92.4	72.0
2000...........	76.3	96.4	60.4	76.3	96.7	59.0	77.6	93.6	69.8
2001...........	76.0	95.9	60.2	76.1	96.4	58.9	77.3	92.6	69.7
2002...........	76.1	95.8	60.2	76.3	96.2	59.2	76.9	93.2	68.6
2003...........	75.2	95.7	58.9	75.6	96.2	57.8	74.7	91.4	67.0
2004...........	74.4	95.7	57.5	74.9	96.3	56.8	74.7	91.0	66.4
2005...........	74.8	95.5	58.4	75.1	96.4	57.2	74.7	90.6	67.0
2006...........	75.8	95.5	60.2	76.2	96.2	59.3	75.0	90.6	67.2
2007...........	75.6	95.9	59.2	76.0	96.4	58.3	74.8	92.8	65.7
2008...........	76.1	95.7	60.4	76.4	96.2	59.4	75.0	92.4	66.7
2009...........	76.1	95.0	61.1	76.6	95.5	60.5	74.5	90.2	66.6
2010...........	75.7	94.7	60.7	76.4	95.7	60.3	74.2	91.0	65.6
2011...........	75.7	94.7	60.6	76.1	95.3	60.0	75.0	89.2	67.5

See note at end of table.

Table 11. **Labor force participation rates by presence and age of youngest child, sex, race, and Hispanic or Latino ethnicity, 1994–2011 annual averages—Continued**

(Percent)

Year	Asian			Hispanic or Latino ethnicity		
	Total	Men	Women	Total	Men	Women
With no children under 18 years						
1994............	—	—	—	62.3	71.5	51.5
1995............	—	—	—	61.2	70.9	50.2
1996............	—	—	—	61.6	71.3	50.5
1997............	—	—	—	62.6	72.1	51.4
1998............	—	—	—	62.8	72.1	51.7
1999............	—	—	—	62.5	71.6	52.2
2000............	—	—	—	63.7	73.2	52.6
2001............	—	—	—	63.0	72.4	52.6
2002............	61.2	67.8	55.0	63.9	72.7	53.2
2003............	59.7	66.4	53.7	62.8	72.1	51.5
2004............	59.1	65.0	53.5	63.5	72.6	52.5
2005............	59.9	66.0	54.3	63.0	72.1	51.9
2006............	60.0	66.2	54.1	63.7	73.0	52.2
2007............	60.2	66.6	54.0	63.7	72.8	52.4
2008............	60.3	66.6	54.4	63.5	72.7	52.1
2009............	59.0	65.3	53.1	62.6	70.7	52.8
2010............	58.1	64.3	52.4	62.0	69.8	52.3
2011............	58.0	63.9	52.6	60.8	68.3	51.6
With children under 18 years						
1994............	—	—	—	70.2	92.1	54.7
1995............	—	—	—	71.0	92.2	55.6
1996............	—	—	—	72.3	93.7	56.7
1997............	—	—	—	74.0	93.4	59.6
1998............	—	—	—	74.2	92.9	60.2
1999............	—	—	—	74.6	93.8	60.3
2000............	—	—	—	75.7	93.8	62.0
2001............	—	—	—	75.7	93.6	62.0
2002............	78.3	93.2	66.6	75.8	93.2	62.7
2003............	78.9	93.5	67.0	75.1	93.4	61.2
2004............	77.9	93.8	64.9	74.9	93.9	60.4
2005............	77.9	93.1	65.6	74.5	94.2	59.6
2006............	78.3	93.2	66.3	75.3	94.2	60.9
2007............	78.9	93.1	67.1	76.5	94.8	61.4
2008............	80.0	93.0	68.8	76.4	94.4	61.4
2009............	80.1	94.1	68.0	76.5	94.2	61.5
2010............	78.2	92.2	66.2	76.6	93.9	62.1
2011............	78.3	93.0	65.4	76.1	93.5	61.8

See note at end of table.

Table 11. **Labor force participation rates by presence and age of youngest child, sex, race, and Hispanic or Latino ethnicity, 1994–2011 annual averages—Continued**

(Percent)

Year	Asian			Hispanic or Latino ethnicity		
	Total	Men	Women	Total	Men	Women
With children 6 to 17 years, none younger						
1994............	—	—	—	74.9	89.7	64.5
1995............	—	—	—	75.4	89.7	65.5
1996............	—	—	—	77.3	92.3	66.7
1997............	—	—	—	77.6	91.2	68.2
1998............	—	—	—	77.5	90.6	68.1
1999............	—	—	—	78.6	91.2	69.5
2000............	—	—	—	79.3	91.5	70.5
2001............	—	—	—	79.6	91.7	70.9
2002............	82.6	91.6	75.7	79.0	91.1	70.2
2003............	82.9	93.5	74.3	78.8	91.5	69.4
2004............	82.6	93.8	73.4	79.6	92.8	70.2
2005............	80.7	92.3	71.2	78.8	92.9	68.7
2006............	80.8	91.8	72.0	79.1	92.6	69.4
2007............	81.8	91.7	73.6	80.5	93.1	70.4
2008............	82.7	91.8	74.9	80.4	93.2	70.0
2009............	82.7	92.9	74.0	80.7	93.6	69.9
2010............	81.8	92.2	73.1	80.1	92.6	69.9
2011............	80.8	92.2	71.2	79.2	91.9	69.0
With children under 6 years						
1994............	—	—	—	66.6	94.0	47.0
1995............	—	—	—	67.6	94.1	47.7
1996............	—	—	—	68.5	94.8	48.7
1997............	—	—	—	70.9	95.1	52.3
1998............	—	—	—	71.3	94.9	53.0
1999............	—	—	—	71.2	95.9	52.1
2000............	—	—	—	72.5	95.7	54.5
2001............	—	—	—	72.2	95.2	53.8
2002............	73.5	94.8	56.3	73.1	94.8	56.1
2003............	74.2	93.4	58.5	71.9	94.9	53.4
2004............	73.1	93.8	56.0	70.6	94.8	51.2
2005............	74.9	94.0	59.3	70.6	95.4	50.9
2006............	75.6	94.8	59.9	71.7	95.6	52.7
2007............	75.8	94.8	59.9	72.9	96.1	53.0
2008............	77.1	94.3	61.9	72.7	95.5	53.0
2009............	77.3	95.4	61.4	72.4	94.9	53.1
2010............	74.3	92.2	58.3	73.2	95.2	54.6
2011............	75.4	93.8	58.4	73.2	95.0	54.7

See note at end of table.

Table 11. **Labor force participation rates by presence and age of youngest child, sex, race, and Hispanic or Latino ethnicity, 1994–2011 annual averages—Continued**

(Percent)

Year	Asian			Hispanic or Latino ethnicity		
	Total	Men	Women	Total	Men	Women
	With children under 3 years					
1994............	—	—	—	64.4	94.1	42.2
1995............	—	—	—	65.7	94.1	43.7
1996............	—	—	—	66.2	94.6	44.7
1997............	—	—	—	68.6	94.6	48.0
1998............	—	—	—	69.5	95.0	48.9
1999............	—	—	—	68.8	96.2	47.4
2000............	—	—	—	70.4	96.2	50.0
2001............	—	—	—	69.7	95.3	48.7
2002............	72.1	95.4	53.5	70.3	95.1	50.3
2003............	73.0	94.5	55.1	69.5	95.2	47.9
2004............	70.2	93.8	50.4	68.2	95.2	46.0
2005............	72.4	92.9	55.8	67.7	96.0	45.0
2006............	73.4	94.2	56.8	69.5	95.9	48.6
2007............	73.6	94.2	56.2	69.9	96.0	47.6
2008............	75.9	94.4	59.5	70.3	95.9	47.9
2009............	76.1	95.9	58.2	70.0	94.4	49.1
2010............	72.2	91.2	55.3	71.3	95.3	50.8
2011............	73.8	95.3	54.1	71.3	95.5	50.1

NOTE: Beginning in 2003, estimates for White, Black or African American, and Asian race groups include people who selected that race group only; people who selected more than one race are not included in these groups. Prior to 2003, people who reported more than one race were included in the group they identified as their main race. Asian estimates for 2002 include Asians and Pacific Islanders; beginning in 2003, Asian is a separate category. People whose ethnicity is identified as Hispanic or Latino may be of any race. Children are "own" children and include sons, daughters, stepchildren, and adopted children. Not included are nieces, nephews, grandchildren, and other related and unrelated children. Dash indicates data not available.

Table 12. **Unemployment rates by sex, race, and Hispanic or Latino ethnicity, 1972–2011 annual averages**

(Percent)

Year	Total			White			Black or African American			Asian			Hispanic or Latino ethnicity		
	Total	Men	Women	Total	Men	Women	Total	Men	Women	Total	Men	Women	Total	Men	Women
1972	5.6	5.0	6.6	5.1	4.5	5.9	10.4	9.3	11.8	—	—	—	—	—	—
1973	4.9	4.2	6.0	4.3	3.8	5.3	9.4	8.0	11.1	—	—	—	7.5	6.7	9.0
1974	5.6	4.9	6.7	5.0	4.4	6.1	10.5	9.8	11.3	—	—	—	8.1	7.3	9.4
1975	8.5	7.9	9.3	7.8	7.2	8.6	14.8	14.8	14.8	—	—	—	12.2	11.4	13.5
1976	7.7	7.1	8.6	7.0	6.4	7.9	14.0	13.7	14.3	—	—	—	11.5	10.8	12.7
1977	7.1	6.3	8.2	6.2	5.5	7.3	14.0	13.3	14.9	—	—	—	10.1	9.0	11.9
1978	6.1	5.3	7.2	5.2	4.6	6.2	12.8	11.8	13.8	—	—	—	9.1	7.7	11.3
1979	5.8	5.1	6.8	5.1	4.5	5.9	12.3	11.4	13.3	—	—	—	8.3	7.0	10.3
1980	7.1	6.9	7.4	6.3	6.1	6.5	14.3	14.5	14.0	—	—	—	10.1	9.7	10.7
1981	7.6	7.4	7.9	6.7	6.5	6.9	15.6	15.7	15.6	—	—	—	10.4	10.2	10.8
1982	9.7	9.9	9.4	8.6	8.8	8.3	18.9	20.1	17.6	—	—	—	13.8	13.6	14.1
1983	9.6	9.9	9.2	8.4	8.8	7.9	19.5	20.3	18.6	—	—	—	13.7	13.6	13.8
1984	7.5	7.4	7.6	6.5	6.4	6.5	15.9	16.4	15.4	—	—	—	10.7	10.5	11.1
1985	7.2	7.0	7.4	6.2	6.1	6.4	15.1	15.3	14.9	—	—	—	10.5	10.2	11.0
1986	7.0	6.9	7.1	6.0	6.0	6.1	14.5	14.8	14.2	—	—	—	10.6	10.5	10.8
1987	6.2	6.2	6.2	5.3	5.4	5.2	13.0	12.7	13.2	—	—	—	8.8	8.7	8.9
1988	5.5	5.5	5.6	4.7	4.7	4.7	11.7	11.7	11.7	—	—	—	8.2	8.1	8.3
1989	5.3	5.2	5.4	4.5	4.5	4.5	11.4	11.5	11.4	—	—	—	8.0	7.6	8.8
1990	5.6	5.7	5.5	4.8	4.9	4.7	11.4	11.9	10.9	—	—	—	8.2	8.0	8.4
1991	6.8	7.2	6.4	6.1	6.5	5.6	12.5	13.0	12.0	—	—	—	10.0	10.3	9.6
1992	7.5	7.9	7.0	6.6	7.0	6.1	14.2	15.2	13.2	—	—	—	11.6	11.7	11.4
1993	6.9	7.2	6.6	6.1	6.3	5.7	13.0	13.8	12.1	—	—	—	10.8	10.6	11.0
1994	6.1	6.2	6.0	5.3	5.4	5.2	11.5	12.0	11.0	—	—	—	9.9	9.4	10.7
1995	5.6	5.6	5.6	4.9	4.9	4.8	10.4	10.6	10.2	—	—	—	9.3	8.8	10.0
1996	5.4	5.4	5.4	4.7	4.7	4.7	10.5	11.1	10.0	—	—	—	8.9	7.9	10.2
1997	4.9	4.9	5.0	4.2	4.2	4.2	10.0	10.2	9.9	—	—	—	7.7	7.0	8.9
1998	4.5	4.4	4.6	3.9	3.9	3.9	8.9	8.9	9.0	—	—	—	7.2	6.4	8.2
1999	4.2	4.1	4.3	3.7	3.6	3.8	8.0	8.2	7.8	—	—	—	6.4	5.6	7.6
2000	4.0	3.9	4.1	3.5	3.4	3.6	7.6	8.0	7.1	3.6	3.6	3.6	5.7	5.0	6.8
2001	4.7	4.8	4.7	4.2	4.2	4.1	8.6	9.3	8.1	4.5	4.5	4.4	6.6	5.9	7.5
2002	5.8	5.9	5.6	5.1	5.3	4.9	10.2	10.7	9.8	5.9	6.1	5.7	7.5	7.2	8.0
2003	6.0	6.3	5.7	5.2	5.6	4.8	10.8	11.6	10.2	6.0	6.2	5.7	7.7	7.2	8.4
2004	5.5	5.6	5.4	4.8	5.0	4.7	10.4	11.1	9.8	4.4	4.5	4.3	7.0	6.5	7.6
2005	5.1	5.1	5.1	4.4	4.4	4.4	10.0	10.5	9.5	4.0	4.0	3.9	6.0	5.4	6.9
2006	4.6	4.6	4.6	4.0	4.0	4.0	8.9	9.5	8.4	3.0	3.0	3.1	5.2	4.8	5.9
2007	4.6	4.7	4.5	4.1	4.2	4.0	8.3	9.1	7.5	3.2	3.1	3.4	5.6	5.3	6.1
2008	5.8	6.1	5.4	5.2	5.5	4.9	10.1	11.4	8.9	4.0	4.1	3.7	7.6	7.6	7.7
2009	9.3	10.3	8.1	8.5	9.4	7.3	14.8	17.5	12.4	7.3	7.9	6.6	12.1	12.5	11.5
2010	9.6	10.5	8.6	8.7	9.6	7.7	16.0	18.4	13.8	7.5	7.8	7.1	12.5	12.7	12.3
2011	8.9	9.4	8.5	7.9	8.3	7.5	15.8	17.8	14.1	7.0	6.8	7.3	11.5	11.2	11.8

See note at end of table.

Table 12. **Unemployment rates by sex, race, and Hispanic or Latino ethnicity, 1972–2011 annual averages—Continued**

(Percent)

Year	American Indian and Alaska Native			Native Hawaiian and Other Pacific Islander			Two or more races		
	Total	Men	Women	Total	Men	Women	Total	Men	Women
2003	10.5	11.2	9.6	7.7	6.9	8.6	9.1	9.3	8.9
2004	9.6	9.7	9.4	6.1	6.8	5.4	8.7	8.7	8.7
2005	9.3	8.7	10.1	4.3	4.8	3.9	8.0	7.9	8.2
2006	7.9	7.9	8.0	5.3	6.3	4.3	6.7	7.3	6.0
2007	8.1	7.9	8.4	4.8	5.4	4.3	7.1	7.4	6.8
2008	9.9	10.8	8.8	6.4	7.7	4.9	9.5	10.1	8.7
2009	13.3	15.5	10.8	10.8	11.6	10.0	13.6	14.2	12.9
2010	15.1	17.3	12.7	12.0	13.6	10.4	13.6	14.2	13.0
2011	14.6	15.4	13.7	10.4	11.4	9.3	13.6	14.0	13.1

NOTE: Beginning in 2003, estimates for White, Black or African American, Asian, American Indian and Alaska Native, and Native Hawaiian and Other Pacific Islander race groups include people who selected that race group only; people who selected more than one race group are included in the two or more races category. Prior to 2003, people who reported more than one race were included in the group they identified as their main race. Asian estimates for 2000–2002 include Asians and Pacific Islanders; beginning in 2003, Asian is a separate category, as is Native Hawaiian and Other Pacific Islander. People whose ethnicity is identified as Hispanic or Latino may be of any race. Dash indicates data not available.

Table 13. **Unemployed people by duration of unemployment, sex, race, and Hispanic or Latino ethnicity, 2011 annual averages**

Duration of unemployment	Total	White	Black or African American	Asian	Hispanic or Latino ethnicity
Total, 16 years and older (thousands)	13,747	9,889	2,831	518	2,629
Percent	100.0	100.0	100.0	100.0	100.0
Less than 5 weeks	19.5	21.1	14.6	16.7	21.2
5 to 14 weeks	21.8	22.4	20.2	19.1	23.5
15 to 26 weeks	15.0	14.8	15.7	14.4	15.4
27 weeks and over	43.8	41.7	49.5	49.9	39.9
Average (mean) duration, in weeks[1]	39.3	37.8	43.3	47.6	36.4
Median duration, in weeks	21.4	19.7	27.0	27.7	18.5
Men, 16 years and older (thousands)	7,684	5,631	1,502	269	1,527
Percent	100.0	100.0	100.0	100.0	100.0
Less than 5 weeks	19.4	21.0	14.4	15.9	21.9
5 to 14 weeks	21.4	22.0	19.9	19.9	23.7
15 to 26 weeks	15.1	14.9	16.1	14.3	15.5
27 weeks and over	44.1	42.1	49.6	49.9	38.9
Average (mean) duration, in weeks[1]	40.0	38.6	43.1	49.8	35.4
Median duration, in weeks	21.7	20.1	27.1	27.7	17.8
Women, 16 years and older (thousands)	6,063	4,257	1,329	250	1,102
Percent	100.0	100.0	100.0	100.0	100.0
Less than 5 weeks	19.6	21.2	14.8	17.5	20.3
5 to 14 weeks	22.2	22.9	20.5	18.1	23.3
15 to 26 weeks	14.8	14.7	15.2	14.5	15.2
27 weeks and over	43.3	41.2	49.5	49.8	41.3
Average (mean) duration, in weeks[1]	38.5	36.7	43.6	45.3	37.7
Median duration, in weeks	21.1	19.2	27.0	27.7	19.6

[1] Beginning in January 2011, this series reflects a change to the collection of data on unemployment duration. For more information, see **http://www.bls.gov/cps/duration.htm**.

NOTE: Estimates for the above race groups (White, Black or African American, and Asian) do not sum to totals because data are not presented for all races. People whose ethnicity is identified as Hispanic or Latino may be of any race.

Table 14. Unemployed people by reason for unemployment, sex, race, and Hispanic or Latino ethnicity, 2011 annual averages

Reason for unemployment	Total	White	Black or African American	Asian	Hispanic or Latino ethnicity
Total, 16 years and older (thousands)	13,747	9,889	2,831	518	2,629
Percent	100.0	100.0	100.0	100.0	100.0
Job losers and persons who completed temporary jobs	59.0	60.7	55.2	53.1	59.7
On temporary layoff	8.9	10.3	5.1	6.3	9.9
Not on temporary layoff	50.0	50.5	50.1	46.8	49.8
Permanent job losers	39.9	40.6	38.7	40.2	37.4
Persons who completed temporary jobs	10.1	9.9	11.4	6.5	12.5
Job leavers	7.0	7.4	5.4	7.4	5.4
Reentrants	24.7	23.4	28.3	26.8	24.2
New entrants	9.3	8.5	11.1	12.7	10.8
Men, 16 years and older (thousands)	7,684	5,631	1,502	269	1,527
Percent	100.0	100.0	100.0	100.0	100.0
Job losers and persons who completed temporary jobs	64.6	66.6	60.4	54.3	67.3
On temporary layoff	10.5	12.1	5.6	5.9	12.1
Not on temporary layoff	54.1	54.4	54.9	48.3	55.1
Permanent job losers	42.3	42.8	41.7	41.3	40.5
Persons who completed temporary jobs	11.8	11.6	13.2	7.4	14.7
Job leavers	6.4	6.7	4.5	9.3	4.9
Reentrants	20.1	18.7	23.8	23.8	17.9
New entrants	8.8	7.9	11.3	12.6	9.9
Women, 16 years and older (thousands)	6,063	4,257	1,329	250	1,102
Percent	100.0	100.0	100.0	100.0	100.0
Job losers and persons who completed temporary jobs	51.8	52.9	49.4	51.6	49.2
On temporary layoff	6.9	7.8	4.6	6.4	6.7
Not on temporary layoff	44.8	45.2	44.8	44.8	42.5
Permanent job losers	36.9	37.6	35.3	39.2	33.0
Persons who completed temporary jobs	7.9	7.6	9.5	5.6	9.4
Job leavers	7.6	8.2	6.3	5.6	6.1
Reentrants	30.6	29.6	33.3	30.0	32.8
New entrants	10.0	9.3	11.0	12.8	12.1

NOTE: Estimates for the above race groups (White, Black or African American, and Asian) do not sum to totals because data are not presented for all races. People whose ethnicity is identified as Hispanic or Latino may be of any race.

Table 15. **People in the labor force and not in the labor force by selected characteristics, 2011 annual averages**

(Numbers in thousands)

Age, sex, race, and Hispanic or Latino ethnicity	Civilian labor force[1]	Not in the labor force						
		Total	Want a job					Do not want a job now
			Total	Searched for work in previous year, but not in past 4 weeks				
				Total	Marginally attached (available to work now)[2]			
					Total	Discouraged workers[3]	Other[4]	
Total								
Total, 16 years and over	153,617	86,001	6,437	3,169	2,573	989	1,584	79,564
16 to 24 years	20,997	17,201	2,023	1,014	752	222	530	15,177
25 to 54 years	101,744	22,961	2,854	1,551	1,289	519	770	20,107
55 years and over	30,876	45,839	1,560	605	532	248	284	44,280
Men, 16 years and over	81,975	34,343	3,045	1,582	1,346	579	767	31,298
16 to 24 years	10,996	8,430	1,069	543	424	136	288	7,360
25 to 54 years	54,638	6,970	1,235	736	651	303	348	5,734
55 years and over	16,341	18,943	740	302	271	140	131	18,203
Women, 16 years and over	71,642	51,658	3,392	1,587	1,227	410	817	48,266
16 to 24 years	10,001	8,771	954	471	328	86	242	7,817
25 to 54 years	47,105	15,991	1,618	814	638	216	422	14,373
55 years and over	14,536	26,896	819	303	261	108	152	26,077
White								
Total, 16 years and over	124,579	68,498	4,624	2,201	1,768	652	1,116	63,874
16 to 24 years	16,834	12,546	1,427	692	501	144	357	11,119
25 to 54 years	81,381	17,311	1,979	1,048	861	329	532	15,332
55 years and over	26,363	38,641	1,218	461	406	179	227	37,423
Men, 16 years and over	67,551	27,249	2,209	1,118	935	385	550	25,041
16 to 24 years	8,926	6,169	764	378	288	89	200	5,405
25 to 54 years	44,502	4,972	856	504	436	194	242	4,116
55 years and over	14,123	16,108	589	236	210	102	108	15,519
Women, 16 years and over	57,028	41,248	2,415	1,083	833	267	566	38,833
16 to 24 years	7,909	6,377	663	314	213	56	157	5,714
25 to 54 years	36,879	12,339	1,123	544	425	135	290	11,216
55 years and over	12,240	22,533	629	226	195	77	119	21,903
Black or African American								
Total, 16 years and over	17,881	11,233	1,243	681	585	261	324	9,989
16 to 24 years	2,752	3,009	425	240	194	66	127	2,584
25 to 54 years	12,420	3,539	595	348	309	148	161	2,944
55 years and over	2,710	4,685	223	92	83	47	36	4,461
Men, 16 years and over	8,454	4,710	574	331	302	153	149	4,136
16 to 24 years	1,342	1,451	214	123	104	40	64	1,237
25 to 54 years	5,872	1,397	264	165	157	86	71	1,133
55 years and over	1,240	1,862	96	44	41	26	15	1,766
Women, 16 years and over	9,427	6,523	669	350	284	108	175	5,853
16 to 24 years	1,410	1,559	211	117	90	26	64	1,347
25 to 54 years	6,547	2,142	331	184	152	61	90	1,811
55 years and over	1,470	2,822	127	49	42	21	21	2,695

See notes at end of table.

Table 15. People in the labor force and not in the labor force by selected characteristics, 2011 annual averages—Continued

(Numbers in thousands)

Age, sex, race, and Hispanic or Latino ethnicity	Civilian labor force[1]	Not in the labor force						
		Total	Want a job					Do not want a job now
			Total	Searched for work in previous year, but not in past 4 weeks				
				Total	Marginally attached (available to work now)[2]			
					Total	Discouraged workers[3]	Other[4]	
Asian								
Total, 16 years and over	7,386	4,054	320	159	118	48	71	3,734
16 to 24 years	659	932	70	33	22	5	17	862
25 to 54 years	5,428	1,360	172	90	66	26	41	1,188
55 years and over	1,298	1,761	78	35	30	17	13	1,684
Men, 16 years and over	3,972	1,457	144	72	57	26	32	1,314
16 to 24 years	336	467	41	17	12	3	9	427
25 to 54 years	2,936	319	68	39	32	13	18	251
55 years and over	700	671	35	15	14	9	5	636
Women, 16 years and over	3,414	2,596	176	87	61	22	39	2,420
16 to 24 years	323	465	30	15	10	2	8	435
25 to 54 years	2,493	1,041	104	51	35	12	23	937
55 years and over	598	1,090	43	20	16	8	8	1,048
Hispanic or Latino ethnicity								
Total, 16 years and over	22,898	11,540	1,101	528	426	180	246	10,439
16 to 24 years	3,982	3,617	410	186	140	48	93	3,208
25 to 54 years	16,390	4,234	539	277	229	102	127	3,695
55 years and over	2,525	3,689	153	65	57	30	27	3,536
Men, 16 years and over	13,576	4,177	481	251	214	101	112	3,696
16 to 24 years	2,357	1,733	209	93	75	29	46	1,524
25 to 54 years	9,803	996	206	124	109	54	54	790
55 years and over	1,416	1,449	67	34	30	18	12	1,382
Women, 16 years and over	9,322	7,363	620	277	212	78	134	6,743
16 to 24 years	1,625	1,884	201	93	65	19	47	1,683
25 to 54 years	6,587	3,238	333	153	120	47	72	2,905
55 years and over	1,110	2,241	86	30	27	12	15	2,154

[1] The sum of the employed plus the unemployed.

[2] People "marginally attached to the labor force" are those who want a job, have searched for work during the prior 12 months, and were available to take a job during the reference week, but had not looked for work in the past 4 weeks.

[3] Discouraged workers are people marginally attached to the labor force who did not actively look for work in the prior 4 weeks for reasons such as thinks no work available, could not find work, lacks schooling or training, employer thinks too young or old, and other types of discrimination.

[4] Includes those who did not actively look for work in the prior 4 weeks for such reasons as child-care and transportation problems, as well as a small number for which reason for nonparticipation was not ascertained.

NOTE: Estimates for the above race groups (White, Black or African American, and Asian) do not sum to totals because data are not presented for all races. People whose ethnicity is identified as Hispanic or Latino may be of any race.

Table 16. **Median usual weekly earnings of full-time wage and salary workers by sex, race, and Hispanic or Latino ethnicity, 1979–2011 annual averages**

Years	Total	White	Black or African American	Asian	Hispanic or Latino ethnicity
	Total, both sexes				
1979....................	$241	$248	$199	—	$194
1980....................	262	269	212	—	209
1981....................	284	291	235	—	223
1982....................	302	310	245	—	240
1983....................	313	320	261	—	250
1984....................	326	336	269	—	259
1985....................	344	356	277	—	270
1986....................	359	371	291	—	277
1987....................	374	384	301	—	285
1988....................	385	395	314	—	290
1989....................	399	409	319	—	298
1990....................	412	424	329	—	304
1991....................	426	442	348	—	312
1992....................	440	458	357	—	321
1993....................	459	475	369	—	331
1994....................	467	484	371	—	324
1995....................	479	494	383	—	329
1996....................	490	506	387	—	339
1997....................	503	519	400	—	351
1998....................	523	545	426	—	370
1999....................	549	573	445	—	385
2000....................	576	590	474	$615	399
2001....................	596	610	491	639	417
2002....................	608	623	498	658	424
2003....................	620	636	514	693	440
2004....................	638	657	525	708	456
2005....................	651	672	520	753	471
2006....................	671	690	554	784	486
2007....................	695	716	569	830	503
2008....................	722	742	589	861	529
2009....................	739	757	601	880	541
2010....................	747	765	611	855	535
2011....................	756	775	615	866	549

See note at end of table.

Table 16. **Median usual weekly earnings of full-time wage and salary workers by sex, race, and Hispanic or Latino ethnicity, 1979–2011 annual averages—Continued**

Years	Total	White	Black or African American	Asian	Hispanic or Latino ethnicity
			Men		
1979.....................	$292	$298	$227	—	$219
1980.....................	313	320	244	—	234
1981.....................	340	350	268	—	251
1982.....................	364	375	278	—	269
1983.....................	379	387	294	—	274
1984.....................	392	401	303	—	287
1985.....................	407	418	305	—	296
1986.....................	419	433	319	—	299
1987.....................	434	450	327	—	306
1988.....................	449	465	348	—	308
1989.....................	468	482	348	—	315
1990.....................	481	494	361	—	318
1991.....................	493	506	375	—	323
1992.....................	501	514	380	—	339
1993.....................	510	524	392	—	346
1994.....................	522	547	400	—	343
1995.....................	538	566	411	—	350
1996.....................	557	580	412	—	356
1997.....................	579	595	432	—	371
1998.....................	598	615	468	—	390
1999.....................	618	638	488	—	406
2000.....................	641	662	510	$685	417
2001.....................	670	689	529	732	440
2002.....................	679	702	524	756	451
2003.....................	695	715	555	772	464
2004.....................	713	732	569	802	480
2005.....................	722	743	559	825	489
2006.....................	743	761	591	882	505
2007.....................	766	788	600	936	520
2008.....................	798	825	620	966	559
2009.....................	819	845	621	952	569
2010.....................	824	850	633	936	560
2011.....................	832	856	653	970	571

See note at end of table.

Table 16. **Median usual weekly earnings of full-time wage and salary workers by sex, race, and Hispanic or Latino ethnicity, 1979–2011 annual averages—Continued**

Years	Total	White	Black or African American	Asian	Hispanic or Latino ethnicity
			Women		
1979....................	$182	$184	$169	—	$157
1980....................	201	203	185	—	172
1981....................	219	221	206	—	190
1982....................	239	242	217	—	203
1983....................	252	254	232	—	215
1984....................	265	268	241	—	223
1985....................	277	281	252	—	230
1986....................	291	294	264	—	241
1987....................	303	307	276	—	251
1988....................	315	318	288	—	260
1989....................	328	334	301	—	269
1990....................	346	353	308	—	278
1991....................	366	373	323	—	292
1992....................	380	387	335	—	302
1993....................	393	401	348	—	313
1994....................	399	408	346	—	305
1995....................	406	415	355	—	305
1996....................	418	428	362	—	316
1997....................	431	444	375	—	318
1998....................	456	468	400	—	337
1999....................	473	483	409	—	348
2000....................	493	502	429	$547	366
2001....................	512	522	454	563	388
2002....................	529	547	473	566	397
2003....................	552	567	491	598	410
2004....................	573	584	505	613	419
2005....................	585	596	499	665	429
2006....................	600	609	519	699	440
2007....................	614	626	533	731	473
2008....................	638	654	554	753	501
2009....................	657	669	582	779	509
2010....................	669	684	592	773	508
2011....................	684	703	595	751	518

See note at end of table.

Table 16. **Median usual weekly earnings of full-time wage and salary workers by sex, race, and Hispanic or Latino ethnicity, 1979–2011 annual averages—Continued**

Years	Total	White	Black or African American	Asian	Hispanic or Latino ethnicity
	Women's earnings as a percentage of men's				
1979..................	62.3	61.7	74.4	—	71.7
1980..................	64.2	63.4	75.8	—	73.5
1981..................	64.4	63.1	76.9	—	75.7
1982..................	65.7	64.5	78.1	—	75.5
1983..................	66.5	65.6	78.9	—	78.5
1984..................	67.6	66.8	79.5	—	77.7
1985..................	68.1	67.2	82.6	—	77.7
1986..................	69.5	67.9	82.8	—	80.6
1987..................	69.8	68.2	84.4	—	82.0
1988..................	70.2	68.4	82.8	—	84.4
1989..................	70.1	69.3	86.5	—	85.4
1990..................	71.9	71.5	85.3	—	87.4
1991..................	74.2	73.7	86.1	—	90.4
1992..................	75.8	75.3	88.2	—	89.1
1993..................	77.1	76.5	88.8	—	90.5
1994..................	76.4	74.6	86.5	—	88.9
1995..................	75.5	73.3	86.4	—	87.1
1996..................	75.0	73.8	87.9	—	88.8
1997..................	74.4	74.6	86.8	—	85.7
1998..................	76.3	76.1	85.5	—	86.4
1999..................	76.5	75.7	83.8	—	85.7
2000..................	76.9	75.8	84.1	79.9	87.8
2001..................	76.4	75.8	85.8	76.9	88.2
2002..................	77.9	77.9	90.3	74.9	88.0
2003..................	79.4	79.3	88.5	77.5	88.4
2004..................	80.4	79.8	88.8	76.4	87.3
2005..................	81.0	80.2	89.3	80.6	87.7
2006..................	80.8	80.0	87.8	79.3	87.1
2007..................	80.2	79.4	88.8	78.1	91.0
2008..................	79.9	79.3	89.4	78.0	89.6
2009..................	80.2	79.2	93.7	81.8	89.5
2010..................	81.2	80.5	93.5	82.6	90.7
2011..................	82.2	82.1	91.1	77.4	90.7

NOTE: Beginning in 2003, estimates for White, Black or African American, and Asian race groups include people who selected that race group only; people who selected more than one race are not included in these groups. Prior to 2003, people who reported more than one race were included in the group they identified as their main race. Asian estimates for 2000–2002 include Asians and Pacific Islanders; beginning in 2003, Asian is a separate category. People whose ethnicity is identified as Hispanic or Latino may be of any race. Dash indicates data not available.

Table 17. **Median usual weekly earnings of full-time wage and salary workers by educational attainment, sex, race, and Hispanic or Latino ethnicity, 2011 annual averages**

Educational attainment and sex	Total	White	Black or African American	Asian	Hispanic or Latino ethnicity
Total, 25 years and older	$797	$825	$643	$901	$582
Less than a high school diploma	451	458	416	448	419
High school graduates, no college[1]	638	663	538	564	568
Some college, no degree	719	743	611	710	643
Associate degree	768	795	624	713	706
Bachelor's degree and higher[2]	1,150	1,165	958	1,224	1,000
Men, 25 years and older	886	909	689	1,006	600
Less than a high school diploma	488	494	447	472	450
High school graduates, no college[1]	720	745	598	615	606
Some college, no degree	818	848	681	772	709
Associate degree	880	909	705	773	784
Bachelor's degree and higher[2]	1,332	1,353	1,027	1,367	1,114
Women, 25 years and older	718	736	613	769	543
Less than a high school diploma	395	394	385	417	377
High school graduates, no college[1]	554	572	493	519	501
Some college, no degree	622	641	578	618	589
Associate degree	682	704	603	656	618
Bachelor's degree and higher[2]	998	1,011	915	1,037	922

[1] Includes people with a high school diploma or equivalent.

[2] Includes people with bachelor's, master's, professional, and doctoral degrees.

NOTE: People whose ethnicity is identified as Hispanic or Latino may be of any race.

Table 18. **Median usual weekly earnings of full-time wage and salary workers by occupation, sex, race, and Hispanic or Latino ethnicity, 2011 annual averages**

Occupation	Total	White	Black or African American	Asian	Hispanic or Latino ethnicity
Total, 16 years and older	$756	$775	$615	$866	$549
Management, professional, and related occupations	1,082	1,103	876	1,268	908
Management, business, and financial operations occupations	1,160	1,175	945	1,261	937
Management occupations	1,237	1,256	968	1,345	953
Business and financial operations occupations	1,038	1,047	912	1,194	906
Professional and related occupations	1,029	1,041	824	1,272	887
Computer and mathematical occupations	1,305	1,298	934	1,474	1,129
Architecture and engineering occupations	1,315	1,326	1,051	1,372	1,108
Life, physical, and social science occupations	1,108	1,121	998	1,150	943
Community and social service occupations	813	828	766	921	778
Legal occupations	1,277	1,331	1,006	1,533	924
Education, training, and library occupations	919	932	807	1,000	836
Arts, design, entertainment, sports, and media occupations	929	928	859	1,161	802
Healthcare practitioner and technical occupations	995	1,011	777	1,120	892
Service occupations	486	491	459	501	421
Healthcare support occupations	487	494	467	511	484
Protective service occupations	757	806	603	790	726
Food preparation and serving related occupations	409	409	388	485	391
Building and grounds cleaning and maintenance occupations	465	465	447	544	403
Personal care and service occupations	453	455	436	474	417
Sales and office occupations	638	651	571	689	559
Sales and related occupations	670	703	507	621	515
Office and administrative support occupations	623	627	589	712	578
Natural resources, construction, and maintenance occupations	732	738	659	743	524
Farming, fishing, and forestry occupations	430	430	476	408	398
Construction and extraction occupations	717	723	628	773	524
Installation, maintenance, and repair occupations	806	813	718	750	671
Production, transportation, and material moving occupations	609	622	569	527	499
Production occupations	605	624	522	526	491
Transportation and material moving occupations	614	619	604	533	509

See note at end of table.

Table 18. **Median usual weekly earnings of full-time wage and salary workers by occupation, sex, race, and Hispanic or Latino ethnicity, 2011 annual averages—Continued**

Occupation	Total	White	Black or African American	Asian	Hispanic or Latino ethnicity
Men, 16 years and older	$832	$856	$653	$970	$571
Management, professional, and related occupations	1,269	1,294	965	1,414	1,019
Management, business, and financial operations occupations	1,370	1,393	1,044	1,434	1,026
Management occupations	1,427	1,447	1,136	1,451	1,002
Business and financial operations occupations	1,225	1,240	990	1,373	1,127
Professional and related occupations	1,211	1,225	912	1,403	1,012
Computer and mathematical occupations	1,369	1,362	861	1,550	1,190
Architecture and engineering occupations	1,343	1,350	1,047	1,407	1,111
Life, physical, and social science occupations	1,156	1,151	1,104	1,248	904
Community and social service occupations	906	939	760	979	893
Legal occupations	1,758	1,791	1,427	1,470	1,294
Education, training, and library occupations	1,109	1,129	915	1,167	981
Arts, design, entertainment, sports, and media occupations	995	987	967	1,350	897
Healthcare practitioner and technical occupations	1,129	1,162	775	1,135	963
Service occupations	551	568	501	535	444
Healthcare support occupations	521	537	492	611	565
Protective service occupations	797	840	632	817	725
Food preparation and serving related occupations	429	424	413	494	402
Building and grounds cleaning and maintenance occupations	502	504	489	544	416
Personal care and service occupations	562	575	509	588	557
Sales and office occupations	738	760	593	751	596
Sales and related occupations	804	839	603	772	619
Office and administrative support occupations	668	679	579	741	583
Natural resources, construction, and maintenance occupations	740	746	663	756	533
Farming, fishing, and forestry occupations	445	444	496	513	410
Construction and extraction occupations	718	726	625	755	524
Installation, maintenance, and repair occupations	807	814	718	762	676
Production, transportation, and material moving occupations	651	667	595	584	525
Production occupations	667	685	556	593	522
Transportation and material moving occupations	634	643	619	540	531

See note at end of table.

53

Table 18. **Median usual weekly earnings of full-time wage and salary workers by occupation, sex, race, and Hispanic or Latino ethnicity, 2011 annual averages—Continued**

Occupation	Total	White	Black or African American	Asian	Hispanic or Latino ethnicity
Women, 16 years and older	$684	$703	$595	$751	$518
Management, professional, and related occupations	941	948	825	1,122	818
Management, business, and financial operations occupations	977	985	889	1,131	847
Management occupations	1,018	1,032	916	1,179	880
Business and financial operations occupations	937	937	854	1,100	819
Professional and related occupations	919	928	796	1,115	806
Computer and mathematical occupations	1,126	1,121	1,002	1,232	858
Architecture and engineering occupations	1,140	1,114	1,136	1,228	1,071
Life, physical, and social science occupations	1,038	1,078	772	1,036	1,170
Community and social service occupations	772	769	768	906	704
Legal occupations	1,003	1,017	919	1,542	847
Education, training, and library occupations	869	881	785	907	772
Arts, design, entertainment, sports, and media occupations	856	857	775	956	727
Healthcare practitioner and technical occupations	965	977	777	1,116	869
Service occupations	433	432	432	480	402
Healthcare support occupations	483	490	462	499	479
Protective service occupations	602	631	583	556	729
Food preparation and serving related occupations	390	393	363	467	367
Building and grounds cleaning and maintenance occupations	406	399	420	544	382
Personal care and service occupations	422	422	423	426	390
Sales and office occupations	602	608	561	637	527
Sales and related occupations	549	578	442	538	437
Office and administrative support occupations	615	618	590	694	576
Natural resources, construction, and maintenance occupations	515	513	552	503	379
Farming, fishing, and forestry occupations	371	366	432	324	348
Construction and extraction occupations	612	585	669	974	487
Installation, maintenance, and repair occupations	751	770	664	588	607
Production, transportation, and material moving occupations	485	486	490	461	405
Production occupations	483	488	473	459	413
Transportation and material moving occupations	490	478	517	526	377

NOTE: People whose ethnicity is identified as Hispanic or Latino may be of any race. Effective with January 2011 data, occupations reflect the introduction of the 2010 Census occupational classification system, derived from the 2010 Standard Occupational Classification (SOC). No historical data have been revised. Data for 2011 are not strictly comparable with data for earlier years. More information about the change in classification is available online at **http://www.bls.gov/cps/documentation.htm#oi**.

Technical note

The estimates in this report were obtained from the Current Population Survey (CPS), a national monthly sample survey of approximately 60,000 eligible households that provides a wide range of information on the labor force, employment, and unemployment. Earnings data are collected from one-fourth of the CPS monthly sample. The survey is conducted for the U.S. Bureau of Labor Statistics (BLS) by the U.S. Census Bureau, using a scientifically selected national sample with coverage in all 50 states and the District of Columbia.

Material in this report is in the public domain and, with appropriate credit, may be reproduced without permission. This information is available to sensory-impaired individuals upon request. Voice phone: (202) 691-5200; Federal Relay Service: (800) 877-8339.

Concepts and definitions

Civilian noninstitutional population. Included are persons 16 years of age and older residing in the 50 states and the District of Columbia who are not confined to institutions, such as nursing homes and prisons, and who are not on active duty in the Armed Forces.

Employed persons. All persons who, during the reference week, (a) did any work at all (at least 1 hour) as paid employees; worked in their own business, profession, or on their own farm; or worked 15 hours or more as unpaid workers in an enterprise operated by a member of the family; and (b) all those who were not working but who had jobs or businesses from which they were temporarily absent because of vacation, illness, bad weather, childcare problems, maternity or paternity leave, labor-management dispute, job training, or other family or personal reasons, whether or not they were paid for the time off or were seeking other jobs.

Unemployed persons. All persons who had no employment during the reference week, were available for work (except for temporary illness), and had made specific efforts to find employment sometime during the 4-week period ending with the reference week. Persons who were waiting to be recalled to a job from which they had been laid off need not have been looking for work to be classified as unemployed.

Duration of unemployment. This represents the length of time (through the reference week) that persons classified as unemployed had been looking for work. For persons on layoff, duration of unemployment represents the number of full weeks they had been on layoff. Mean duration is the arithmetic average computed from single weeks of unemployment; median duration is the midpoint of a distribution of weeks of unemployment.

Reason for unemployment. Unemployment also is categorized according to the status of individuals at the time they began to look for work. The reasons for unemployment are divided into four major groups:

(1) Job losers, comprising (a) persons on temporary layoff, who have been given a date to return to work or who expect to return within 6 months (persons on layoff need not be looking for work to qualify as unemployed), (b) permanent job losers, whose employment ended involuntarily and who began looking for work, and (c) persons who completed temporary jobs, who began looking for work after the jobs ended.

(2) Job leavers, persons who quit or otherwise terminated their employment voluntarily and immediately began looking for work.

(3) Reentrants, persons who previously worked but who were out of the labor force prior to beginning their job search.

(4) New entrants, persons who had never worked.

Labor force. This group comprises all persons classified as employed or unemployed in accordance with the criteria described above.

Unemployment rate. This represents the number of unemployed persons as a percentage of the labor force.

Participation rate. This represents the proportion of the population that is in the labor force.

Employment-population ratio. This represents the proportion of the population that is employed.

Not in the labor force. Included in this group are all persons in the civilian noninstitutional population who are neither employed nor unemployed. Persons marginally attached to the labor force are those individuals who are not in the labor force who wanted and were available for work and had looked for a job sometime in the prior 12 months (or since the end of their last job if they held one within the past 12 months). They were not counted as unemployed because they had not searched for work in the 4 weeks preceding the survey. Discouraged workers, a subset of the marginally attached, were not looking for work because they believed no jobs were available for them.

Occupation and industry. This information applies to the job held during the reference week. People with two or more jobs are classified in the occupation and industry in which they worked the greatest number of hours. The occupational and industry classification of CPS data is based on the 2010 Census Occupational Classification system and the 2007 Census Industrial Classification system, which are derived from the 2010 Standard Occupation Classification (SOC) and the 2007 North American Industry Classification (NAICS). More information about these classifications are available online at the following website **http://www.bls.gov/cps/cpsoccind.htm**.

White, Black or African American, Asian, American Indian and Alaska Native, and Native Hawaiian and Other Pacific Islander. In accordance with the Office of Management and Budget guidelines, these are terms used to describe the race of persons. Beginning in 2003, persons in these categories are those who selected that race group only. Those who identify multiple race groups are categorized as persons of two or more races. (Previously, persons identified a group as their main race.) Estimates for Asians, American Indians and Alaska Natives, Native Hawaiians and Other Pacific Islanders, and persons of two or more races are not shown separately in all tables because the number of survey respondents is too small to develop estimates of sufficient quality. In the enumeration process, race is determined by the household respondent. More information on the 2003 changes to questions on race and Hispanic ethnicity is available at **http://www.bls.gov/cps/rvcps03.pdf**.

Hispanic or Latino ethnicity. This refers to persons who identified themselves in the enumeration process as being Spanish, Hispanic, or Latino. Persons whose ethnicity is identified as Hispanic or Latino may be of any race. More information on the 2003 changes in questions on race and Hispanic ethnicity is available at **http://www.bls.gov/cps/rvcps03.pdf**.

Usual weekly earnings. Data represent earnings before taxes and other deductions, and include any overtime pay, commissions, or tips usually received (at the main job, in the case of multiple jobholders). Earnings reported on a basis other than weekly (for example, annual, monthly, hourly) are converted

to weekly. The term "usual" is as perceived by the respondent. If the respondent asks for a definition of usual, interviewers are instructed to define the term as more than half the weeks worked during the past 4 or 5 months. Data refer to the sole or primary job of wage and salary workers (excluding all self-employed persons regardless of whether their businesses were incorporated).

Median earnings. These figures indicate the value that divides the earnings distribution into two equal parts, one part having values above the median and the other having values below the median. The medians shown in this publication are calculated by linear interpolation of the $50 centered interval within which each median falls.

Family. A family is defined as a group of two or more persons residing together who are related by birth, marriage, or adoption; all such persons are considered as members of one family. Families are classified either as married-couple families or as families maintained by women or men without spouses.

Children. Data on children refer to one's own children and include sons, daughters, stepchildren, and adopted children. Not included are nieces, nephews, grandchildren, other related children, and all unrelated children living in the household.

Reliability of the estimates

Statistics based on the CPS are subject to both sampling and nonsampling error. When a sample, rather than an entire population, is surveyed, there is a chance that the sample estimates may differ from the "true" population values they represent. The exact difference, or sampling error, varies depending on the particular sample selected, and this variability is measured by the standard error of the estimate. There is about a 90- percent chance, or level of confidence, that an estimate based on a sample will differ by no more than 1.6 standard errors from the "true" population value because of sampling error. BLS analyses are generally conducted at the 90- percent level of confidence.

All other types of error are referred to as nonsampling error. Nonsampling error can occur for many reasons, including the failure to sample a segment of the population, inability to obtain information for all respondents in the sample, inability or unwillingness of respondents to provide correct information, and errors made in the collection or processing of data. More information on the reliability of data from the CPS and estimating standard errors is available at **http://www.bls.gov/cps/documentation.htm#reliability**.